S0-CFS-871

... Evans Picture Library); Christine Osinski: 5 bottom, 119; Corbis Images: 8 (John Henley), cover, 2, 3 (Royalty-Free), 93 (Stephen Welstead/LWA); Getty Images: 61 (Peter Cade/Stone), 59 (Fernanda Calfat), 14 (The Image Bank/White Cross Productions); Index Stock Imagery/Omni Photo Communications Inc.: 22; JupiterImages: 17, 56 (Bananastock), 117 (Creatas Images), 37 (Goodshoot), 50 (image 100); Mandometer Clinic, San Diego, CA: 103; Mirrorpix: 73; Photo Researchers, NY: 6 (Oscar Burriel), 44 (Richard T. Nowitz), 99 (Ed Young); PhotoEdit: 33 (Bob Daemmrich), 4, 27 (Tony Freeman); photolibrary.com: 112 (Image100), 21 (Plainpicture), cover inset (Veer Incorporated-Fancy); Phototake: 5 top, 77 (Laurent/Di Pasquale), 107 (Yoav Levy); Remuda Ranch Programs for Eating Disorders: 105; Richard Hutchings Photography: 68; Superstock, Inc./age fotostock: 108; The Image Works/Bob Daemmrich: 80.

Book design by The Design Lab

Library of Congress Cataloging-in-Publication Data
Orr, Tamra.
    When the mirror lies : anorexia, bulimia, and other eating disorders / by Tamra Orr.
        p. cm.
    Includes index.
    ISBN-10: 0-531-16791-7 (lib. bdg.)
    ISBN-13: 978-0-531-16791-5 (lib. bdg.)
    ISBN-10: 0-531-17977-X (pbk.)
    ISBN-13: 978-0-531-17977-2 (pbk.)
    1. Body image in adolescence—Juvenile literature. 2. Eating disorders in adolescence—Juvenile literature. 3. Self-perception—Juvenile literature. I. Title.
    RJ506.E18O77 2006
    618.92'8526—dc22   2005025571

Dedication: To the amazing young men and women who shared their personal and powerful stories with me. I have never been so touched and so honored to glimpse such strength and bravery.

WHEN THE MIRROR
LIES

ANOREXIA, BULIMIA, AND OTHER EATING DISORDERS

BY TAMRA B. ORR

Note to the reader: All the stories used in this book are true. They are honest looks at what happened to men and women who found themselves with eating disorders. Sprinkled throughout this book are lots of sidebars. The Chapter Menus let you know what you will be learning in each chapter. The Weighty Words are quotes that are worth thinking about for a while. Little Bites are statistics and facts that just may surprise—or even shock—you. Food for Thought gives you questions to ponder about yourself, your friends, and your classmates.

A Division of Scholastic Inc.
New York • Toronto • London • Auckland • Sydney
Mexico City • New Delhi • Hong Kong
Danbury, Connecticut

TABLE OF CONTENTS

WEIGHTY WORDS

*"To suppress the most basic of needs is to strangle oneself—
more slowly, but no less effectively than poison,
a blade to the artery, a bullet aimed at the brain."* [1]

INTRODUCTION

OBEYING THE VOICE

RINGGGGGGG! The alarm clock goes off at 6:30 A.M. sharp, but you've already been awake for at least an hour. You can't sleep very well anymore, and besides, you are just too cold to relax. You're never warm anymore, even if it is summertime.

People with eating disorders may spend a lot of time in front of a mirror obsessing about how they look.

You slowly and carefully rise out of bed. If you move too fast, the world starts to fade away into a gray fog. You don't want to faint like you did last week. It scared you and gave you a huge bruise on your hip that was hard to explain in physical education class. You check to see if there are any clumps of hair on your pillow. If your mom sees it, she will suspect something.

Your arms and legs hurt a little less today. Sometimes they ache so fiercely you are afraid that someone will notice you wincing. You look down at your forearms, pleased at how you can see your wrist bones standing up so clear and sharp. You can remember a day a few months ago when they were covered in sickening layers of fat. Your happiness disappears quickly, however, as you examine the area above your elbows. No matter how many times you lift weights, you cannot get your upper arms to look anything but disgustingly thick and ugly. With a growing dread, you approach the mirror in your bedroom and strip off your pajamas. You take a long look at your naked body, going inch by inch, from head to toe. You turn and scrutinize it from every possible angle. The longer you look, the angrier you get. The Voice in your head suddenly shifts from a soft whisper to a piercing scream.

"You're repulsive. You're still fat. No breakfast today. You don't deserve it.

No one will be able to look at you in school today because you are just too hideous. How gross!"

As you descend the stairs, the smell of frying bacon meets you, and you can't help but take a deep breath. It smells so wonderful. You remember long-ago breakfasts of crisp bacon, hot scrambled eggs, and toast swimming in melted butter. "Forget it, little girl! You don't get a bite and you know it. Where's your self-control?" The Voice is back.

9

You sigh and put on a false smile and enter the kitchen. "I'm running late, Mom," you say, staggering under the weight of your backpack. "No time to eat. Sorry!"

"Take your lunch then," reminds your mother, thrusting a sack at you.

"I'm going out with friends," you say, backing out of the front door and leaving the sack on the kitchen table. You keep your eyes off of the bacon.

Finally.

You're safe.
You're in control.
You start to feel the power.
It only lasts a second.

"Stop being lazy. Start running," the Voice says. You take a deep breath and start jogging down the sidewalk. Maybe, just maybe, if you can run the two miles extra fast, you can have some nonfat yogurt for lunch.

"Don't count on it," sneers the Voice. "If you do, you know what you will have to do later."

The idea of vomiting for the third day in a row is just too much to bear. The smell. The sound. The burning in your throat. Forget it. It's easier to just skip lunch. Maybe just some water before first period. It has to be cold. That uses up more calories.

"Stop thinking and speed up!" shouts the Voice. "Remember, no pain, no gain!"

UNDERSTANDING THE VOICE

Hopefully, the Voice in this story has never been anywhere near your head. It is the seductive and devious voice of an eating disorder, and it is the driving force behind millions of people in this country starving themselves to become as thin as possible—sometimes to the point of death. It is a voice that turns people into walking skeletons or, for bulimics, unstoppable eaters.

For many of us, it is impossible to imagine what it would be like to have food become the enemy. It is like being told that oxygen is not good for you, so just stop breathing for an hour or so. How can you do that?

But the victims of eating disorders battle food issues every single day. There are no drive-through meals, quick snacks, family dinners, or meals out with friends. Food is no longer a normal part of life; it's an abnormal, ever-present threat. These men and women learn to ignore overwhelming hunger. They are fascinated by food and often read recipes, bake, and watch cooking shows—yet they refuse to eat. If they do give in to food, they punish themselves. They exercise to exhaustion, or they fast the next day. They only hold on to the food for minutes and then give it right back—at a very high physical cost.

Eating disorders affect between five million and ten million young people in the United States today. Knowing how so many developed these disorders—following their footsteps, mapping their routes, and seeing their challenges—might help to keep their numbers from growing.

CHAPTER MENU

In this chapter you will:

- *Read the stories of Sammie and Patricia*
- *Discover the top-ten myths about eating disorders*
- *Find out about the prevalence of eating disorders in the United States*
- *Learn how eating disorders are diagnosed*
- *Find out what activity disorder is*

CHAPTER ONE

WHO IS THAT IN THE MIRROR?

SAMMIE'S STORY A new school. New people. How to fit in? These are the dilemmas that thirteen-year-old Sammie found herself facing as she started junior high school. She had been struggling with body issues for as long as she could remember. "No one is happy with how they look in today's society," she says. "Models are tall and skinny like Barbie." Why not look like them? That is precisely what Sammie set out to do.

Making friends and fitting in at school can be stressful, especially for someone struggling with an eating disorder.

"I was about 10 or 15 pounds (4.5 or 6.8 kilograms) overweight, and I lost it and then I kept going," says Sammie. At 5 feet 4 inches (163 centimeters) tall, Sammie started out at about 135 pounds (61 kg). It was not long before she was only 87 pounds (39 kg). "I would have kept going, but my parents put me in the hospital," she recalls. "I no longer had the strength to ask them not to do it." Sammie's family life played a large role in her condition.

14

For eight years, her parents had been together and then separated over and over, and she felt like she was right in the middle of it all. "I was taking care of them instead of them taking care of me," she says.

"I think I stopped eating in part to say, 'Hey! Look at me!' "

In addition, her mother is a "workout fiend," according to Sammie. "She is obsessed with it and cannot go a day without it. She would often leave her child—me—just so she could go and work out." Sammie followed her mom's example and began exercising often as well. In addition, she was purging on a regular basis. "I read books about **anorexia**, but they didn't help me," she admits. "On really bad days, I would be so freezing cold—beyond cold. I thought I would never be warm again. I would sit by the radiator for hours and feel so empty."

RECOVERY

By the time she was admitted to the hospital, Sammie's heart rate had dropped to less than forty beats per minute (normal heart rate is 60 to 80 beats per minute). She had to have a feeding tube inserted to keep her alive. "I was put in the psychiatric hospital for two months and was on and off antidepressants." It was not fun for anyone.

"The fear of having a feeding tube put into my nose was like a knife stabbing me in my heart," says Sammie. "They put it in, and I pulled it out. They finally threatened to tie my arms down, and I panicked."

Terrified of gaining weight, Sammie stuck pierced earring posts in her feeding tube so the liquid would leak out rather than go into her.

"I would rather have died. It was the hardest, most painful thing I have ever gone through. It isn't like having a broken arm and getting a cast so you can heal. You can't get away from this," she confesses.

Sammie is seventeen years old now and a junior in high school. She is still struggling to maintain her weight. She is in therapy and knows that what she is doing is the right thing, even if it is hard. "I know that if I have the control to not eat, I have the control to eat," she assures. "Eating disorders do not solve anything, and you hurt people more than you could ever imagine. You have to learn to accept who you are, and life is too short to keep running away. Eventually, you still have to deal with everything you were avoiding before. I went into the hospital kicking, screaming, crying, and telling my parents I hated them. Now I know I can never thank them enough."[1]

LITTLE **BITES:** *The average American woman is 5 foot 4 (163 cm) and weighs 140 pounds (64 kg). The average American model is 5 foot 11 (180 cm) and weighs 117 pounds (53 kg).*

SURROUNDED BY FOOD

It is hard to imagine people starving on purpose. Think about what food means in today's culture. Food is a part of socializing. Hanging out with friends usually means pizza, potato chips, or some other food. Being at home means sitting around the table or television and sharing dinner. Many holidays are linked with food. What is Thanksgiving without turkey? What is Halloween without candy? What is a birthday without cake? What is Christmas without cookies? What is Valentine's Day without chocolate? In addition, we tend to associate food with our emotions. Prepping for a hard test? Load up on snack food. Feeling sick? Time for chicken noodle soup. Hard day? Grab some cookies from Mom. Depressed? Bring on the chocolate. Just got dumped? Where is the ice cream?

who IS that in the mirror?

17

Despite all this, between five and ten million people in this country are struggling to do something that most of us take for granted every day: eat.

While we sit down to a meal, grab a snack, or munch on a treat—often without giving it much, if any, thought—millions of boys and girls, men and women are too frightened, too threatened, too obsessed to do the same. They may restrict their calories tightly through enormous self-control or feel that control slip away and begin binging and purging. They are victims of eating disorders, psychological disorders that turn basic nutrition into a lethal weapon.

THE MYTHS OF EATING DISORDERS

Myths surround almost any topic you can think of, and eating disorders are no exception. Read these statements. Which of them do you think are true?

✳ **Everyone who has an eating disorder comes from a dysfunctional family. Usually there is a domineering mother and a passive father.** *While eating disorders do affect kids with family issues, they occur just as often in families in which the parents are kind, loving, and concerned.*

✳ **You can never completely recover from an eating disorder.** *It is entirely possible to recover from anorexia or bulimia. The personal stories in this book prove that.*

✳ **Compulsive overeating is a matter of willpower and is not a type of eating disorder.** *Overeating is not as simple as a matter of willpower. Those with eating disorders often have more willpower than the average person. It is far more like an addiction.*

✳ **Eating disorders are just a problem with how much food a person does or does not eat.** *The focus of eating disorders seems to be food, but issues with eating are only symptoms of the disease, not the cause. Most experts believe that eating disorders are all about self-esteem, control, and body image.*

19

MYTHS

✳ **No one dies from an eating disorder.** *People die from the complications of eating disorders—too many people. Statistics show that with treatment, 2 to 3 percent die. Without treatment, that number climbs to 20 percent.*

✳ **People only binge on sweets.** *When you think of someone binging, it may seem like it is always on foods like ice cream or cookies. But many people binge on healthy foods, including fruits and vegetables. Binge eating is not about what a person eats but how much and in what way.*

✳ **You can have bulimia or anorexia but not both.** *A study done by the American Journal of Psychiatry in April 2005 demonstrated that 36 percent of patients with anorexia developed bulimia and 27 percent of those with bulimia developed anorexia, most within five years of the onset of their illness.*

✳ **Only upper-class, wealthy white girls get eating disorders.** *Eating disorders aren't biased. They don't discriminate. They hit boys, girls, whites, blacks, Asians, Latinos. They can attack you if you are poor, middle class, or wealthy.*

✳ **People who binge always purge. Purging is always done by vomiting.** *Some people who binge also purge. Others just binge. This is often referred to as compulsive overeating. Purging is more than vomiting. It can also mean using* **diuretics***, medication, exercise, or* **laxatives** *to get rid of food and waste.*

WEIGHTY WORDS

"Anorexia is to dieting as decapitation is to a paper cut." [2]

LITTLE BITES: *There are three billion women who don't look like supermodels and only eight who do.*[3]

How prevalent are eating disorders? Currently, almost nine million females and one million males have been diagnosed. Here is the breakdown for girls:

PREVALENCE OF EATING DISORDERS

Anorexia Nervosa
0.25 to 1 percent of middle- and high-school girls
Bulimia Nervosa
1 to 3 percent of middle- and high-school girls
1 to 4 percent of college women
1 to 2 percent in community samples
Atypical Eating Disorders
(following fad diets, overeating)
3 to 6 percent among middle-school girls
2 to 13 percent among high-school girls

AGE OF ONSET

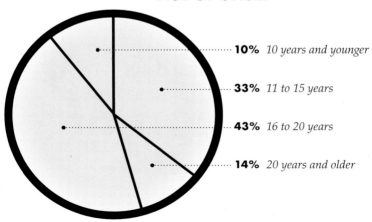

10% *10 years and younger*

33% *11 to 15 years*

43% *16 to 20 years*

14% *20 years and older*

(*From* "Disordered Eating Past and Present," *by Marc Darrow, MD, JD, in* The Eating Disorders Sourcebook)

23

who IS that in the mirror?

LEARNING THE LINGO

What distinguishes one eating disorder from another? There are official definitions in medical books, but here are the basics.

Anorexia Nervosa

The word anorexia actually means "without **appetite.**"

In reality, anorexics are always hungry. The hunger never goes away. It may be suppressed, ignored, and overpowered, but it does not go away.

The word nervosa means **"condition of the mind."**

Here are some telltale signs doctors look for as they try to make a diagnosis:

SYMPTOMS OF AN EATING DISORDER

✳ **Fifteen percent or more under normal weight.** *If you are a female and 5 foot 2 (157 cm), your lowest recommended weight is 102 pounds (46 kg). If you weigh less than 87 pounds (39 kg), you meet this standard. If you are a male and 5 foot 7 (170 cm), your lowest recommended weight is 138 pounds (63 kg). If you weigh less than 117 pounds (53 kg), you also meet this standard.*

✳ **An intense fear of gaining weight.** *The key here is the word* intense. *If you are bummed because the dance is this weekend and your favorite jeans are too tight to wear, that is normal. If you are throwing up, taking laxatives and diuretics, and are emotionally distraught about your weight, that is abnormal. Do you have nightmares about getting fat? Do you look at other people and see them as disgustingly overweight? Does the idea of gaining weight make you panic? If so, this is a strong sign of a potential problem.*

✳ **A distorted body image.** *What happens when you look in the mirror? If you are like most of us, you notice that while you certainly have some areas that could use some improvement, you won't keep staring at them hatefully for hours. You can give an honest assessment of how you appear. This is your overall body image. It has been forming since the day you first looked in a mirror and is influenced by everyone from your family to friends to the media. Those with eating disorders can't look in the mirror and do the same kind of assessment. They see a deformed and distorted reflection, even though the rest of the world does not see it at all.*

25

who IS that in the mirror?

SIGNS OF A BODY IMAGE PROBLEM

The Renfrew Center Foundation is an organization in Philadelphia, Pennsylvania, that works for the prevention, education, research, and treatment of eating disorders. In their booklet, "Understanding Body Image Problems," they list the following criteria that may signal a body image problem. Ask yourself these questions:

* Are you unable to accept a compliment?
* Is your mood affected by how you think you look?
* Do you constantly compare yourself to others?
* Do you call yourself disparaging names such as "fat," "ugly," or "gross"?
* Do you try to achieve a "perfect" image?
* Do you repeatedly seek reassurance from others that you look acceptable?
* Do you consistently overestimate the size of your body or body parts?
* Do you think that if you could just attain a goal weight, then you would accept yourself?
* Does your drive to be thin overwhelm all other pleasures or goals?
* Do you think that being thin equals beauty, success, happiness, perfection, and self-control?
* Do you feel connected to your whole body or do you look at it as separate parts?
* Are you terrified of becoming fat?
* Do you feel shame about yourself or your body?

A distorted body image is one of the symptoms of eating disorders.

Amenorrhea

If a girl's **menstrual** periods used to be regular but have now disappeared for at least three months, this is called **amenorrhea** and may be a sign of anorexia. Starving affects a girl's menstrual cycle and can make her periods stop completely. For obvious reasons, this particular symptom does not pertain to boys. Because of this factor, males were often not diagnosed with anorexia for a long time. Yet, anorexia affects levels of **testosterone**, the male hormone, as well.

who IS that in the mirror?

STANDARD WEIGHT CHARTS[4]

MEN

HEIGHT	WEIGHT (small to large frames)
5'2" (157 cm)	128–150 pounds (58–68 kg)
5'3" (160 cm)	130–153 pounds (59–69 kg)
5'4" (163 cm)	132–156 pounds (60–71 kg)
5'5" (165 cm)	134–160 pounds (61–73 kg)
5'6" (168 cm)	136–164 pounds (62–74 kg)
5'7" (170 cm)	138–168 pounds (63–76 kg)
5'8" (173 cm)	140–172 pounds (64–78 kg)
5'9" (175 cm)	142–176 pounds (64–80 kg)
5'10" (178 cm)	144–180 pounds (65–82 kg)
5'11" (180 cm)	146–184 pounds (66–83 kg)
6'0" (183 cm)	149–188 pounds (68–85 kg)
6'1" (185 cm)	152–192 pounds (69–87 kg)
6'2" (188 cm)	155–197 pounds (70–89 kg)
6'3" (191 cm)	158–202 pounds (72–92 kg)
6'4" (193 cm)	162–207 pounds (73–94 kg)

WEIGHTY WORDS

*"A man cannot be too serious about his eating,
for food is the force that binds society together."*

~ Confucius

WOMEN

HEIGHT	WEIGHT (small to large frames)
4'10" (147 cm)	102–131 pounds (46–59 kg)
4'11" (150 cm)	103–134 pounds (47–61 kg)
5'0" (152 cm)	104–137 pounds (47–62 kg)
5'1" (155 cm)	106–140 pounds (48–64 kg)
5'2" (157 cm)	108–143 pounds (49–65 kg)
5'3" (160 cm)	111–147 pounds (50–67 kg)
5'4" (163 cm)	114–151 pounds (52–68 kg)
5'5" (165 cm)	117–155 pounds (53–70 kg)
5'6" (168 cm)	120–159 pounds (54–72 kg)
5'7" (170 cm)	123–163 pounds (56–74 kg)
5'8" (173 cm)	126–167 pounds (57–76 kg)
5'9" (175 cm)	129–170 pounds (59–77 kg)
5'10" (178 cm)	132–173 pounds (60–78 kg)
5'11" (180 cm)	135–176 pounds (61–80 kg)
6'0" (183 cm)	138–179 pounds (63–81 kg)

The word bulimia means having the appetite of an OX.

Bulimia is four to six times more common than anorexia. It is the most common eating disorder of all. After all, this is a way to "have your cake and eat it too." For a person to be diagnosed as a bulimic, the medical books say that he or she must binge and purge at least twice a week for at least three months. This means:

✳ **A lot of food is eaten in one sitting.** *Many of us can admit to a time when we downed an entire pizza, ate all of the cookies in the cookie jar, or polished off the whole potato chip bag. An occasional pigging out isn't real binging because it is just that—occasional. According to statistics, the average bulimic binges 11.7 times a week, although some do it far more often than that.*

A lot of food means a quantity larger than the average person can eat in one sitting. Researchers who have studied bulimic patients state that while the normal person eats about 38.4 calories per minute, a bulimic averages 81.5 calories per minute. A typical binge consumes

3,415 calories (more than most people eat in an entire day and the equivalent of about six Big Macs) but has been reported to hit a high of almost 12,000 calories (or twenty Big Macs).[5]

✳ **The food is eaten very quickly.** *Food is not carefully put on plates, cut into pieces, and chewed thoroughly. It is stuffed into the mouth and swallowed as quickly as possible. The average length of a binging episode is seventy-eight minutes from beginning to end. (Studies have shown it can be over in as little as fifteen minutes or last as long as eight hours.)*

✳ **There is a loss of control; it is impossible to stop.** *Bulimics often report that they feel completely out of control and unable to stop what they are doing long after they are full. The pleasure of eating what they have been denying themselves is fleeting and is quickly followed by guilt, shame, and disgust. Many bulimics will pace or be agitated while eating, and secrecy is common. Embarrassed by their actions, they usually binge alone so no one can see what they are doing.*

✳ **Binging is followed by some form of purging.** *When they are done binging, bulimics purge in some way. They simply can't help it. It's the only way to deal with the revulsion and humiliation they feel for losing control. They may vomit, use laxatives or diuretics, engage in intense, nonstop exercising, or resort to some combination of these methods.*

who IS that in the mirror?

WEIGHTY WORDS

"After years of starvation, my body cried out so urgently for food that I gave in . . . and started a cycle of binging. I ate and ate until I couldn't eat any more, until my stomach hurt. I ate entire boxes of cookies, loaves of bread, a half-gallon of ice cream—anything I could get my hands on. Then the anxiety set in. I remember thinking, What have I just done? I have absolutely no willpower. That was when I had to vomit."[6]

Binge Eating/Compulsive Overeating

Compulsive overeating is binging without purging. A compulsive overeater eats large quantities of food quickly and secretively but does not try to get rid of it afterward. This person often ends up with severe weight problems and is at high risk of developing bulimia.

WEIGHTY WORDS

"Paint me a picture of an eating disorder— it's an emaciated woman. But that's not the reality. They don't get down that low. The face of eating disorders is your next-door neighbor's daughter or maybe your own."[7]

32

You have been taught from as early as you can remember that exercise is good for you. Your mom told you to get off the couch and go outside and play. Your physical education teacher urged you to run faster, jump higher, and reach farther. Your coach holds the stopwatch and records your time, telling you to work harder and practice more. Your family doctor encourages you to ride your bike, shoot some hoops, or chase a ball. So you are absolutely positive that exercise is good for you.

Exercise is an important part of a healthy lifestyle, but regularly exercising past the point of exhaustion can be part of an eating disorder.

33

You are right—if it is done in moderation. Unfortunately, people with eating disorders exercise obsessively in an attempt to force the pounds from their bodies. This mania results in a condition that many psychologists refer to as an activity disorder. It is also known as pathogenic exercise or **anorexia athletica**. Researchers believe that three-quarters of all anorexics and bulimics have some degree of it.[8]

People with activity disorders become addicted to physical exercise. It goes far beyond the regular high you might get from exercise. It is normal to feel exhilarated, excited, and energized from working your body. Exercise releases special chemicals in your brain called **endorphins** and **serotonin**. They are natural drugs that make you feel happy.

The trouble starts when you HAVE to exercise to feel pleasure.

You need it to fight your concern about gaining weight. You need it to bolster your self-esteem. It is part of your focus on self-discipline. Exercise becomes a compulsion that you cannot control.

It does not take long for an activity disorder to drive you to a state of total exhaustion. Your concentration will falter. Your performance in any sport will spiral downward fast. You will be sore and stiff, and you will find yourself falling asleep at odd moments throughout the day. Your response to this?

I don't care if it hurts.

I don't care if I'm tired.

If I rest,

I will get fat.

WEIGHTY WORDS

"There was a time when I felt I was one step away from total annihilation. Everyone, it seemed to me, knew me as the 'golden girl' with the perfect grades, cute figure, bubbly personality, totally in-charge composure, and a future that could only lead to success. How could they ever accept what I really was: sad, insecure, FAT, out of control, and scared that I couldn't hold the facade together much longer? Would they be impressed that I could finish a gallon of ice cream, a dozen doughnuts, and all the Cheetos in the pantry, then pretend to shower while actually regurgitating it all up? Would they think me clever for being able to obtain as much junk food as I did without arousing the suspicion of clerks, roommates or friends? Wait—what friends?"

~ Dr. Lynne Mordant[9]

who IS that in the mirror?

A DISEASE IN DISGUISE?

There are a few medical conditions that can mimic eating disorders and need to be ruled out before an eating disorder diagnosis is made and treatment is arranged. A sudden loss of weight and difficulty eating might also be signs of:

✳ **irritable bowel syndrome**
✳ **inflammatory bowel disease**
✳ **Crohn's disease**
✳ **an endocrine disorder like hypothyroidism or hyperthyroidism**
✳ **diabetes**

It is important to have these other health issues checked out before making a diagnosis of anorexia or bulimia.

WEIGHTY WORDS
"Suicide, when it looks like dieting, just seems to earn you respect." [10]

PATRICIA'S STORY

Patricia met her eating disorder later than many do. She was already grown, in her late twenties, and a mom with two young children when it snuck into her life and made it veer off track.

"I am 5 feet 9 inches (175 cm), and for most of my life, I weighed right about 150 pounds (68 kg)," she recalls. "I was a single mom, working full-time, and very active. I always thought I was fat, so I exercised seven days a week, running and lifting weights.

Not all people with eating disorders are teenagers. Many adults also struggle with these diseases.

37

who IS that in the mirror?

I lost 15 pounds (7 kg) and then gained it back again for several years. Dieting was something I could control, and getting weighed every day was like an addiction. If I saw the numbers shifting, I would panic. My children sensed something wasn't right, but did not know what it was. They were worried and frustrated."

Like others, Patricia went through periods of not eating and then binging. "I would only eat one grape all day, and then I would binge on apples or fruit. Once I ate an entire watermelon and looked like I was eight months pregnant," she says. "I would come home from work, lock the door, and not go out. I was moody and miserable. My weight dropped to 104 pounds (47 kg), my hair was falling out, and my periods stopped. I simply was not myself anymore." Although she wasn't eating, she kept feeding her kids as usual. If friends asked her out, she would simply reply, "Thanks, but I am on a diet." She became a neat freak around the house, cleaning it obsessively. Realizing that she was dealing with an eating disorder, she read everything she could about it. "I wanted to know what the facts were so when someone asked me if I was okay, I could have my defense ready."

Finding Help

While all this was happening, Patricia did see several doctors. "None of them picked up on what was happening to me," she says. "They just noted I had lost a lot of weight. I was silently hoping they would help me. I had no support system at all but suffered this in silence, never telling anyone what I was going through."

"Each night, I felt like I was going to go to sleep and never wake up," she confesses. "I tried to volunteer as a blood donor and my veins kept collapsing. My heart felt like it was struggling to work, and I was so tired, drained. My biggest concern was that my two young children would be the ones to discover my dead body, and the thought of that scared me more than anything else." Finally, she happened to see an article in the local newspaper for a free clinical study about anorexia. "I called to see if I qualified, and I did," recalls Patricia. "I knew it would be discrete, and it was free—and they were willing to help me, so I went for it!"

By being a part of the study, Patricia was compelled to attend meetings more than if she had just had a few doctor's appointments on her own. "I learned to become friends with food for the first time in my life," says Patricia.

Today, almost a decade later, Patricia is maintaining her weight and doesn't even own a scale.

"I threw it in the garbage," she says. "The end result is that you cannot judge your health by weight alone. I no longer own one and instead base my health on how I feel, how I look, and how my overall attitude is—something you can't know just by looking at numbers on a scale."[11]

39

who IS that in the mirror?

CHAPTER MENU

In this chapter you will:

- Read the stories of Catherine and Dorrie
- Find out how self-esteem, self-image, and body image affect eating disorders
- Learn how family environment and dynamics affect eating disorders
- Examine our culture's ideas about beauty and the media's influence on young people
- Learn the major warning signs of a possible body image problem

CHAPTER TWO

BEHIND THE FRACTURED IMAGES

CATHERINE'S STORY This is the first time outside of family and therapy that Catherine has ever shared her story. Although it happened nearly twenty years ago, it is still hard to talk about.

"I was in my senior year at high school, about five months before graduation, when I developed anorexia," she recalls. "It was truly a life-altering event, and it formed who I was."

The women in Catherine's family had struggled with weight issues for a long time. Her mother and aunts were chronic yo-yo dieters. Catherine, however, had no weight problems. "I felt skinny and awkward, all hair and eyes," she says. "My mother made a lot of comments about my thinness, and I remember her telling me, 'Oh, you will have to watch it. You are like us, and one day, you will put on weight.' It was literally branded on my consciousness, and I swore then that I would never be like her.

"And then my awareness of weight went from zero to 60 in 1.5 seconds," she states.

"I became intensely aware of my body and, at the same time, developed an aversion to food."

Catherine's diet was increasingly restrictive. First, she just cut out potato chips, soda, and candy bars. "I began learning the calorie content of all foods," she says. Then she began decreasing her calorie count even further. Her decline was amazingly rapid. "I demanded to see a therapist," she says. "I knew intellectually what was happening."

Catherine was 5 foot 5 (165 cm), and her weight quickly dropped from 120 pounds (54 kg) to 88 pounds (40 kg).

"I was hallucinating, my periods stopped, I grew fuzz all over my body, and I was terribly sensitive to temperature changes. I was terribly depressed."

Frightened, she went to her father, a physician, and asked for help. It wasn't easy. Her parents had been distant and stressed in their relationship with her for as long as she could remember. It came as little surprise when the therapist she began seeing told her that her eating disorder was a family system issue. In hopes of getting better, she tried to bring her parents in for family therapy, but they could not admit to her illness and refused. "I think they were just too focused on their own problems," suggests Catherine.

At her graduation, Catherine was the valedictorian and frighteningly thin. Later, she destroyed all the pictures of her at that time because she could not look at herself that way again.

behind the fractured images

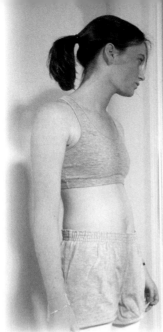

When they look in a mirror, anorexics and bulimics often don't see what other people see.

Moment of Truth

It was not long after she graduated that Catherine went to a party and her life drastically changed. "I looked in the mirror, and for the first time in months, I actually SAW myself," she recalls. "I had spent hours looking at my body before and always thought I needed to lose more weight. This time, however, I was caught unaware by my reflection, and it was as if I saw myself through someone else's eyes. The experience was so intense, I almost vomited," she says. "I was terrified of dying or the thought that I had done irreparable damage to my body. I had this sudden moment of clarity, and it was almost a mystical experience."

Catherine found the therapy that she needed to get her life back. Although she had a brief relapse a year later, today she is a happily married woman who is eager to start her own family. She is also deeply afraid that she did too much damage to her body to be able to have children. She has had three miscarriages in the last eighteen months and is currently in therapy for grief counseling.

"I have to wonder if somehow **I hurt myself** in some way back then," she says in a trembling voice.[1] **If she remains unable to have a baby,** it is a question that will **haunt her.**

LITTLE **BITES:** *Concern about weight and appearance seems to be starting younger and younger. Look at these numbers:*
- *Forty-two percent of first- to third-grade girls want to be thinner.*
- *Fifty percent of nine- and ten-year-olds feel better about themselves if they are on a diet.*
- *Eighty-one percent of ten-year-olds are afraid of being fat.*[2]

45

behind the fractured images

THE HISTORY OF EATING DISORDERS

Eating is a big part of our lives. Many of the things we do at home, school, work, and play involve food in some way or another. Food has been at the center of communities and families throughout history. Feasts were common in ancient Rome, and it was considered an insult to the host if you did not eat to excess.

William Withey Gull was born in 1816 and died in 1890. He received his medical degree from the University of London in 1846.

During the Middle Ages, attitudes began to change. The Catholic Church felt so strongly about overeating, that gluttony became one of the capital sins. Some women stopped eating to show their holiness or faith in God. Their apparent lack of appetite was attributed to a religious miracle, and the condition was later given the name anorexia mirabilis. One woman, who became known as Saint Catherine of Sienna, decided to fast to show her devout belief. It didn't last long. She died at the age of thirty-three.

During the 1870s, doctors finally began to look at eating disorders and put names to what had simply been called "the starving disease." An English physician named Dr. William Withey Gull used the name anorexia for the women he was treating. Another doctor, French neurologist Charles Lasegue, began using the same term in 1873.

It took much longer before bulimia got a name. It was not until 1959 that a psychiatrist named Albert Stunkard wrote the first medical paper on binge eating.[3]

LITTLE **BITES:** *In 1807, an English woman named Ann Moore told everyone that she had decided to quit eating completely. It was not long before people began to pay money to look at her, like the sideshows that once existed in circuses. She made a lot of money before her trick was found out. Her mother was passing food to her by mouth whenever they hugged or kissed.[4]*

behind the fractured images

SEARCHING FOR THE WHO

Profiling or stereotyping people is always dangerous. It can put the spotlight on some who don't deserve it and can overlook those at risk. There are some general traits, however, that those who are caught by anorexia, bulimia, or binge eating appear to have in common. Are these traits an infallible way to recognize a potential victim? No, but they are a general rule to keep in mind.

People dealing with **eating disorders** are often **perfectionists.**

They are often the ones who strive to be the best athletes, students, sons, or daughters. When describing people with eating disorders, Karen Smith, MSS, LSW, founder and director of Full Living, a national education center on eating disorders and body image says, "They are smart, with a drive to succeed." These are the kids who always have their homework done and always get high grades. They may be the captain of the basketball team or the track team. You know the ones. They are the kids you would least suspect of causing or having problems.

But their whole lives are about control. Scheduling time to study, go to practice, and participate in other activities takes an immense amount of self-control and self-discipline—the same traits necessary to maintain an eating disorder.

WEIGHTY WORDS

"If a child asks to go on a diet, parents need to be as conscientious as if the child asked to go on steroids for athletic performance or to take contraceptive pills."

~ Craig Johnson, PhD, past president of the National Eating Disorders Association[5]

Eating disorder patients' lives are about control.

Eating large quantities of food quickly and secretively is one sign of an eating disorder.

LITTLE **BITES:** *Marilyn Monroe wore a size 14 and was considered sexy and beautiful in the 1950s and 1960s. Today, she would be considered a "plus size."*[6]

WATCHING FOR THE SIGNS

The major signs that a person may have an eating disorder are fairly clear. The first ones echo what you already have seen as the symptoms doctors use for a diagnosis of anorexia. They go beyond that, however. Carolyn Costin, MA, MEd MFCC, wrote a paper called "Assessing the Situation." In it, she details many signs that may indicate a person has an eating disorder:

SIGNS OF A POSSIBLE EATING DISORDER

✳ does anything to avoid hunger

✳ avoids eating even when hungry

✳ has a preoccupation/obsession with food

✳ eats large quantities of food in secret

✳ counts calories in all foods eaten

✳ disappears into the bathroom after each meal

✳ feels guilty after eating

✳ is preoccupied with a desire to lose weight

✳ must earn food through excessive exercising

✳ uses exercise as punishment for overeating

✳ is preoccupied with fat in food

✳ avoids entire food groups

✳ eats only diet or nonfat foods

✳ uses products such as laxatives, diuretics, diet pills, caffeine, stimulants, amphetamines, enemas, or ipecac syrup

✳ shows rigid control around food

✳ weighs obsessively

✳ complains of being fat when at normal weight or already too thin

✳ eats when upset

✳ is on and off diets regularly

✳ complains about the appearance of specific body parts

✳ checks the circumference of thighs, particularly when sitting, and space between thighs when standing[7]

51

behind the fractured images

SEARCHING FOR THE WHY

Perhaps the most frustrating part of eating disorders is the inability to point a finger and say, "Look! There is the cause! That's it!" Unlike other medical conditions, no one can determine the precise trigger that makes the difference in a person. It is the same question that many researchers ask about alcoholics. Why can one person drink and be done with it, while the next takes a drink and ends up addicted? No one knows, and it is the same with anorexia and bulimia.

Interviews with those who have gone through an eating disorder show that, for some, it all began with a comment from someone. Perhaps Aunt Mary said you are getting a little plump or your older brother says soon you are going to weigh more than he does. Other times, it may be triggered by a huge life change like a parent's divorce, moving, or someone's death. Approaching puberty and the many physical changes it can bring may set off the problem.

No matter what triggers it, however, it always feeds off of **low self-esteem** and **insecurity.**

LITTLE **BITES:** *Thirty-five percent of normal dieters progress to pathological dieting. Of those, 20 to 25 percent progress to partial- or full-syndrome eating disorders.*[8]

The causes of anorexia and bulimia are complex.

Eating disorders probably result from a combination of many things, including family dynamics, environment, attitudes, personality, and genetics.

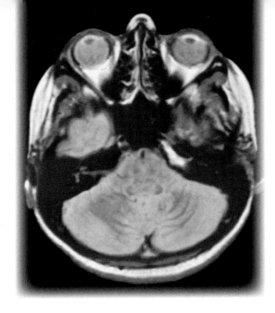

Some researchers use imaging technology to study the brains of eating disorder patients.

RECENT DISCOVERIES

In 1998, researchers at the University of Texas's Southwest Medical Center identified a pair of hormones called orexin A and B. They found that rats injected with orexin ate eight to ten times more food than normal.[9]

In 2001, a Dutch study looked at 145 anorexics and found that 11 percent shared a particular genetic mutation.[10]

In 2002, a medical study reported that eating disorders might be an autoimmune disorder similar to conditions such as multiple sclerosis, lupus, or rheumatoid arthritis. In these health problems, the body attacks its own tissues.[11]

In 2004, brain imaging was done on female anorexics. It showed that the section of the brain that controls and regulates the sensation of pleasure was less active than in non-anorexic women.[12]

While each of these discoveries is interesting and holds promise, they do not hold complete answers or solutions. Eating disorders are, in many ways, similar to other psychological conditions like autism or schizophrenia. Why they happen is rarely clear. All we can do is look at some of the common factors and try to figure it out from there. We can use them to create theories, not answers.

SELF-ESTEEM, SELF-IMAGE, AND BODY IMAGE

Self-esteem is how you feel about yourself. Self-image is your sense of identity. Many things can affect both of these, including your own personal beliefs and values, your parents, your friends, your school, and your job. Your body image is how you look at your body's size and shape. It is hard to remember that not everyone sees your "flaws" the way you do when you look in a mirror. You may see the part of your hair that wouldn't curl right and the pimple under your left ear. No one else does. This tendency to judge ourselves more harshly than we judge others is exaggerated in people who have eating disorders. They look at themselves and see hideous forearms, gigantic thighs, or huge stomachs that aren't really there.

Other people see the real picture— **bones** and emaciation.

Sometimes family dynamics increase the chances that a family member will develop an eating disorder.

FAMILY ENVIRONMENT AND DYNAMICS

Some studies have shown that children growing up in homes where there are very strict rules or rigid expectations have a stronger tendency to developing anorexia or bulimia. In this kind of family, children may feel like they don't have any control over their lives. By developing anorexia or bulimia, however, they can at least control what does and doesn't go into their mouths.

Another family dynamic that can increase the risk of eating disorders is if a parent, particularly the mother, places a lot of emphasis on dieting and exercising. Eating a healthy diet and making exercise a part of life are good things, but too much emphasis on using them to achieve some ideal body shape can be harmful.

LITTLE **BITES:** *Forty-six percent of nine- to eleven-year-olds are "sometimes" or "very often" on diets, and 82 percent of their families are "sometimes" or "very often" on diets.[13]*

BRAIN CHEMISTRY AND GENETICS

Neurotransmitters are chemicals in the brain that act as messengers between the brain and the rest of the body. Serotonin plays a role in sleep, depression, anxiety, and appetite.

Studies have shown that some **anorexics** produce too much **serotonin,** putting them in an ongoing state of **high anxiety.**

Think of how you feel when you are very worried, stressed, or frightened. That is what it can be like to have too much serotonin in your system. What can you do to reduce the amount? Restrict how much you eat. As the chemical drops, you begin to feel more in control again. Studies have also shown that bulimics often have less serotonin than they need. How do they increase it? By binging.

There is little doubt that genetics plays a role in eating disorders. Studies have shown that if one twin develops an eating disorder, the other twin has a 50 percent chance of developing one, too. Also, if a mother or her daughter develops an eating disorder, other girls in the family are twelve times more likely to develop anorexia and four times more likely to become bulimic.[14]

57

behind the fractured images

CULTURAL IDEAS OF BEAUTY AND THE INFLUENCE OF THE MEDIA

A number of researchers have looked at how the media has affected today's ideas of beauty. The ideal woman today is far different than from just a few decades ago. Size 14, once thought to be attractive but now considered by many people to be "plus-sized," is what the average woman wears. The average fashion model, on the other hand, wears a size 4.

Many studies have shown that time spent looking at size 4, airbrushed models in magazines and on television makes women feel less attractive. How can the average girl even attempt to compete with these women? They are perfection. What young people do not see is that these people have been enhanced by personal trainers, makeup crews, skillful camera operators, and the miracle of airbrushing. They are seeing clever disguises that they cannot possibly live up to, no matter how many weights they lift or how many calories they refuse to eat.

Obviously not everyone who sees beauty ads and commercials develops eating disorders. But for those who are already dealing with self-esteem problems, dwelling on these images of false beauty can be a dangerous trigger that pushes them closer to the edge of an eating disorder.

LITTLE **BITES**: *Ninety-one percent of women surveyed on a college campus had attempted to control their weight through dieting, and 22 percent of them dieted "often" or "always."*[15]

WEIGHTY WORDS

*"Supermodels in all the popular magazines have continued to get thinner and thinner. Modeling agencies have been reported to actively pursue anorexic models. The average woman model weighs up to twenty-five percent less than the typical woman and maintains a weight at about fifteen to twenty percent below what is considered healthy for her age and height. Some models go through plastic surgery, some are 'taped-up' to mold their bodies into more photogenic representations of themselves, and photos are airbrushed before going to print. By far, these body types and images are **not the norm and unobtainable** to the average individual, and far and wide, the constant force of these images on society makes us believe they should be. We need to remind ourselves and each other constantly (especially children) that these images are fake."[16]*

IF BARBIE WERE A REAL WOMAN

If she were a real woman, Barbie would have a 39-inch (99 cm) bust, an 18-inch (46 cm) waist, and 33-inch (84 cm) hips. To show how ridiculous and out of proportion that would be, Mandy Golman, an educator, trainer, and consultant on women's wellness issues, came up with a fun project. During Southern Methodist University's annual Eating Disorders Awareness Week, she and the women from her Psychology for Women class built a life-size Barbie doll out of papier-mâché. "We chose her because the Barbie doll is often the first image of what a woman's body should look like for little girls," explains Golman. The finished product was 7 feet (213 cm) tall. "Six of those feet were legs," she adds with a smile. "Her chest was too big for her to be able to stand up at all."

The experience inspired Golman to start a new mentoring program at SMU called Girls in Motion. It lasts for eight weeks, and it gives girls in fourth and fifth grade the chance to meet weekly with a college student for physical exercise. They discuss health and nutrition and even take cooking classes together. The class is so popular there is a waiting list.[17]

WEIGHTY WORDS

"No one can stop the media. We can only inoculate against its virus by recognizing that the bias is there but never let it replace our self-esteem."

~ Dr. David Wall[18]

Many young girls play with fashion dolls such as Barbie.

LITTLE **BITES:** *If Barbie were a real woman, she would have to walk on all fours due to her proportions.*[19]

THE BOTTOM LINE

The causes of eating disorders are unclear, confusing, and complex. The bottom line, in the opinion of many researchers, is that it isn't as important to study why they occur as to figure out how to treat these disorders. The reasons why any one person develops a disorder are individual, a mixture unique to that person. But no matter what the causes are, the effects are devastating to everyone who struggles with anorexia, bulimia, or compulsive overeating. These disorders destroy the body as they carve away at the mind and emotions. It's time to focus on what they do—and how they can be fought.

behind the fractured images

Are Your Eating, Exercise, and Weight Attitudes HEALTHY?

Answer yes or no to the following questions.

YES NO I feel guilty if I eat too much or if I eat foods I think I shouldn't.

YES NO I use diet pills, metabolism-boosting pills, or other weight-loss aids.

YES NO I have been on and off more diets than I can count.

YES NO I am very aware of my intake of fats, carbohydrates, and/or calories.

YES NO I have recently lost and/or gained more than 30 pounds.

YES NO My mood improves when I feel in control of my weight/eating.

YES NO There are certain foods I try to never eat (i.e., fried foods, desserts).

YES NO I hide food or lie to others about how much I actually eat.

YES NO I sometimes feel unable to stop eating once I start.

YES NO There are things I hate about the shape and/or size of my body.

YES NO I use food as a comfort or an escape from my problems.

YES NO   I often skip meals and sometimes go an entire day without eating.

YES NO   My eating and/or exercise patterns are making me somewhat isolated.

YES NO   I have a difficult time identifying or handling my feelings.

YES NO   I spend a great deal of time planning meals and thinking about food.

YES NO   I avoid social situations because I'm ashamed of my eating/weight.

YES NO   I worry about gaining weight or becoming fat.

YES NO   I just don't feel right unless I exercise every day.

YES NO   I sometimes vomit after meals or use laxatives to control my weight.

YES NO   Once I reach my goal weight, then I'll feel good about myself.

If you answered **YES to five or more questions**, then you may have or be at risk of developing an eating disorder.[20]

63

DORRIE'S STORY

Dorrie can remember the exact moment it occurred to her that she needed to go on a diet. "I was ten years old, and I was reading a book about a girl who was being teased because her thighs rubbed together on hot summer days. And I thought, 'Oh no! So do mine!' I panicked. I thought I must be fat, too. I had better lose weight until my thighs don't touch each other."

Since she was not overweight to start with, it was not long before Dorrie was anorexic. She lost more than 20 pounds (9 kg) but hid it from her parents. "I pocketed my lunch money," she says, "and I existed on diet Tab cola." In addition, she began exercising four hours a day. "At first, when my parents noticed it, they thought it was kind of cute, but then they got worried and forbid me to do it anymore." Dorrie's father was a physician who often put his patients on diets, and his advice to his daughter was to eat. So she did. She ate too much too quickly. She gained the weight back and then some. All through middle and high school, she battled being overweight, and her chronic dieting led to low self-esteem and a poor self-image.

"When I was in college, I was binging," recalls Dorrie. "The underlying issues of my food problems had never been addressed." She joined the hockey team and between the stress of classes and being on a team that praised thinness, she began to crumble. "I didn't know the warning signs," she says. "I was in complete denial and never really recognized that I had a problem." Over the summer, she gained more weight, and when she returned to school, she was no longer on the hockey team's starting lineup.

Finding Herself

Binging and purging continued through college, and by the time she got to graduate school, she was also running. Finally, at twenty-three, she went to counseling for the first time and dealt with a lot of tough issues.

"I realized that who I was was just what other people expected me to be," she confesses.

"I was even getting a degree in bioengineering—a field I didn't even like." At the end of her therapy, the symptoms of her eating disorders had subsided, and she was learning more about who she truly was. "I had a PhD, but it was in a profession I didn't care about," she admits. "So I took a month off, and then I went back and got a degree in counseling. That was much more ME," she adds. "It was a journey of self that took ten years."[21]

Today, Dr. Dorrie McCubbrey is a counselor who specializes in eating disorders and has her own treatment center in Boulder, Colorado. She is the author of *How Much Does Your Soul Weigh?*

behind the fractured images

CHAPTER MENU

In this chapter you will:

- ❖ *Read about Jeff and Danny and how they dealt with their eating disorders*
- ❖ *Discover how anorexia and bulimia affect a person's body from head to toe*
- ❖ *Learn how anorexia and bulimia affect a person's mind, emotions, and personality*
- ❖ *Find out how eating disorders affect men*

CHAPTER THREE

RAVAGES INSIDE AND OUT

JEFF'S STORY It all started when he joined the school's track team. "I was in ninth grade, a freshman," says Jeff, "and I really became obsessed with running." It was not long before he also began to restrict his calories and soon the 5-foot-7 (170 cm), 145-pound (66 kg) student had dropped to less than 100 pounds (45 kg). "I figured I could just eat one granola bar a day and keep running," he says.

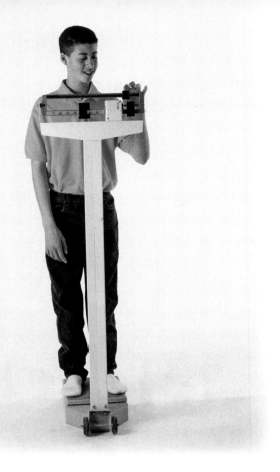

The incidence of eating disorders in young men is on the rise.

Looking back on it now, a few years later, Jeff has a lot of insight into what happened. "It was a weird thing. As a guy, I wasn't as affected by the culture or media like girls often are. I wanted to be strong and athletic. Instead, I just looked bony. I recognized that I was losing a lot of weight, but I just didn't see it as a problem." Neither did most of the people around him.

His parents thought it was a phase at first. Jeff's older brother noticed what was happening but responded by yelling at Jeff and pushing food in his face. "I know he was doing it out of love and because he was frustrated," says Jeff, "but screaming at me that I was a skeleton did not help. It only made me more upset and determined." His track coach didn't say a thing. His friends didn't mention it. His karate teacher simply told him not to come back until he had gained some weight. "It was actually my art teacher who first talked to me about it," recalls Jeff. "I had a good relationship with him, and he had influenced me a lot. He noticed I was quiet and withdrawn and said it was time to bring in my parents."

Jeff's relationship with his friends was faltering, too. "I was sleeping all the time, taking a lot of naps," he recalls. "I really got used to suppressing my hunger, though. Lunch in the school cafeteria was always stressful. I would either avoid it altogether or sit with my friends and watch them eat. I felt really superior.

I knew **I had more self-control** than they did.

If they invited me out to eat, I told them I had already eaten—which was always a lie. Teenage boys are always eating," he adds with a smile, "so my relationships really suffered." Although Jeff did not binge, purge, or use laxatives or diuretics, his calorie level was so restricted that he lost weight rapidly.

ravages inside and out

69

Finding a Way Out

By the beginning of his sophomore year, when Jeff weighed less than 100 pounds (45 kg), he and his parents agreed it was time to go to the hospital and get some help. "I was feeling consumed by the eating disorder, and it was like being split-minded," he describes. "I would go back and forth in my head about what I should do. I was pretty willing to get therapy, although I was hesitant about taking the antidepressants they gave me." Jeff was an inpatient at the Belmont Eating Disorders Facility for a month and an outpatient for several months after that. "I was the only guy there," he admits, "and so yeah, sometimes I felt a little lost in discussions about lost menstrual periods, but watching these women who had suffered for years with an eating disorder really motivated me to get better." Jeff worked with a therapist and a nutritionist and says he got his life back on track quickly. He gives much of the credit for that to others. "Teachers, friends, and family are crucial to recovery," he says. "All of my friends came to the hospital to see me and were very supportive."

During therapy, Jeff learned some of the underlying issues behind his form of anorexia. "I felt like I needed to fulfill everyone's expectations of me," he explains. "I had to be the perfect student, the star athlete—and never, ever disappoint my parents. Limiting food was something I was really successful at." Therapy has helped Jeff to reach realistic goals for himself instead of attempting to be perfect. He is currently getting ready to start his second year in college and is thinking about majoring in neuroscience. His warning words to others? "You can have a much happier life by learning to cope with emotional issues in a way that isn't harmful to your body. Don't ever use food in a way that puts yourself at risk. You can only do what you want to do in life if you are not consumed by food."[1]

You break an arm, it heals. You get a cold, it goes away. When it comes to conditions like anorexia and bulimia, however, it is not that simple.

Eating disorders are illnesses that have the potential to injure the entire body, literally from head to toe.

Very little escapes their ravages, and while some of those effects are temporary, some can be frighteningly permanent. In other words, not everything goes away. Not all of it heals.

ravages inside and out

THE EFFECTS OF ANOREXIA

When a body loses enough weight that it begins to starve, it literally starts feeding on itself for energy. When young men and women look in a mirror and see fat where it doesn't exist, they aren't thinking about what is happening inside of them.

✻ **Muscle tissue begins to waste away.** *After the body has burned all the fat it can, it will begin to burn muscle tissue and, eventually, organs. These can rarely be regained, and damage can be permanent.*

✻ **The body grows an extra layer of hair called lanugo.** *This is the body's attempt to get warmer. It is a fine layer that usually shows up on the face and back of the neck first.[2]*

✻ **Bones lose calcium and begin to get brittle.** *The result is a greater risk for breaks, plus a much higher chance of **osteoporosis**, a condition usually seen in elderly people in which the bones are so fragile that they fracture easily. A recent study of 130 anorexics in their twenties found that 92 percent of them had significant bone loss in their spines and hips. More than a third of them had enough bone loss to be diagnosed with osteoporosis. This bone loss may be permanent.[3]*

* **The intestines slow down.** *They don't work as efficiently because there is so little food and fiber going through them. Also, if a person has become dependent on laxatives, it can interfere with the natural action of the intestines. This creates constipation. Nausea is common.*

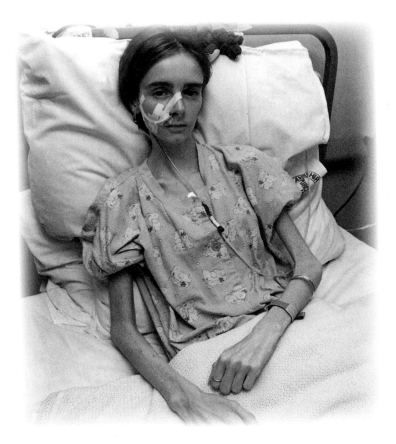

Patients with severe anorexia must be hospitalized to treat the many effects of the disease.

ravages inside and out

✳ **Iron levels drop and anemia sets in.** *Inadequate nutrition creates a number of vitamin and mineral imbalances within the body. When a person doesn't get enough iron, the result is a condition called anemia. A person with anemia is very tired, and fainting and dizziness are common. Other common deficiencies include low levels of sodium and potassium. Each deficiency carries its own side effects and causes damage to the body if left untreated.*

✳ **Core body temperature drops.** *A starving body is unable to maintain a normal temperature of approximately 98.6 degrees Fahrenheit (37 degrees Celsius). The person feels cold and is unable to get warm, despite layers of blankets or clothing. This is a cold that comes from within.*[4]

✳ **Menstrual periods stop.** *When regular menstrual cycles stop, the level of **estrogen** in the body drops. This is the hormone that is responsible for the development of breasts and female reproductive organs. If they are not able to develop normally, it may affect a girl's ability to get pregnant and have children later on in life.*

LITTLE **BITES:** *Americans spend more than $40 billion on dieting and diet-related products each year.*

74

✳ **Internal organs shrink, including the heart and the brain.** *The heart begins to shrink, and the walls get thinner.[5] Blood pressure drops, heartbeat becomes irregular, and the circulation of blood to all the body parts is inhibited. Because the heart begins to pump less effectively, fluid can start collecting in the lungs, a life-threatening condition. Heart failure is one of the leading causes of death for people with eating disorders. The brain also shrinks, and it becomes much harder for the person to concentrate. Comprehension is affected. This occasionally leads to an incorrect diagnosis of attention deficit disorder (ADD).[6]*

✳ **The kidneys begin to malfunction.** *The kidneys' job is to keep the body's fluids balanced and to remove waste from the body. Frequent use of laxatives, diet pills, or both can create problems and may lead to complete kidney failure.*

✳ **Growth and development are interrupted.** *Adolescence is a time when people grow a lot. If nutrition is inadequate, the body will not be able to grow as it was intended to. Growth will slow down and maybe even stop completely.*

✳ **And there are other effects.** *Other health problems from anorexia include pale, yellow, cracked, dry skin; sore, painful joints; irregular sleep patterns; and an impaired immune system that struggles so much that other illnesses take hold and do damage.*

ravages inside and out

75

THE EFFECTS OF BULIMIA

Binging and purging also wreak havoc on the body.

✳ **Tooth decay.** *Repetitive vomiting causes stomach acid to be in the mouth over and over again. This caustic acid destroys the enamel on the teeth and gums and causes teeth to decay.*

✳ **Damaged esophagus.** *Frequent throwing up injures the esophagus. Stomach acid is hard on these tissues. If vomiting is done often enough and hard enough, it can cause the esophagus to tear and rupture. This is a life-threatening situation.*

✳ **Indigestion and stomach pain.** *The stomach is not allowed to function like it is supposed to. First, it has to contend with huge amounts of food; then, before it can digest the food, it is forced to regurgitate it. This causes nausea, bloating, discomfort, indigestion, and pain. If enough damage occurs, a person may begin to vomit blood.*

✳ **Low blood potassium levels.** *Low blood potassium levels can result in a potentially fatal disturbance of the heart's rhythm. The heart can simply stop beating. As a result, the brain doesn't get enough blood. If the disturbance lasts more than a few seconds, permanent brain damage results.*

✳ **Swollen glands.** *The salivary glands become enlarged and sometimes infected. This can make a person look like their cheeks are swollen.*

✳ **Dehydration.** *A lot of water is lost when a person vomits. If it is not replaced, it can lead to an imbalance in **electrolytes** and to dehydration. This can result in irregular heartbeats and possibly death.*

✳ **Other effects.** *Other conditions that go hand in hand with binging and purging include broken blood vessels and stomach ulcers. If a person vomits too often, it is not unusual for them to reach a point where they can never keep any food down, even if they want to.*

Binging and purging on a regular basis can cause stomach pain and other health problems.

ravages inside and out

77

INNER TURMOIL

The physical affects of eating disorders are vicious and pervasive. They affect everything from the hair on your head to poor circulation in your toes. Some can heal and repair with time, others cannot. But the effects go far beyond the physical. Eating disorders are primarily psychological illnesses.

Depression, anxiety, and mood swings are common in those struggling with eating disorders.

Personality changes are common as well. It is not unusual for those who are fighting to avoid eating to be stubborn, aggressive, and frightened. Irrational thinking and poor judgment are always present, from the rationalizing of how many calories the three-mile run earned you to how your butt looks in the mirror. In addition, anorexia and bulimia bring feelings of guilt and shame.

Eating disorder victims often feel so anxious that they experience panic, or anxiety, attacks.

A person who has a panic attack experiences intense feelings of fear and worry. It often comes out of the blue, without warning. You may just be studying, talking to a friend, or walking to the school bus. Suddenly, your heartbeat speeds up and you tremble or feel faint. Your breathing becomes quick and shallow, causing you to **hyperventilate**. You are terrified that you are dying. The attack lasts only a few minutes, but those minutes seem like a lifetime. Afterward, you feel weak and emotionally and physically exhausted.

ravages inside and out

Obsessive-Compulsive Disorder

Eating disorders have also been known to create symptoms of obsessive-compulsive disorder, or OCD. This condition causes your mind to be filled with powerful, unwanted thoughts that drive you to do something repetitively, for instance washing your hands, counting something, turning a light switch on and off, or completing some other kind of ritual.

Compulsive cleaning can be a symptom of obsessive-compulsive disorder.

People with anorexia or bulimia are also at a much higher risk of becoming self-injurers. They may cut or burn themselves intentionally. Pulling their hair, hitting, biting, or scratching themselves can bring about other types of damage. Why do they do it?

It may seem **easier to control the physical pain** than the **emotional pain** that is really at **the root of their problems.**

This is also why many develop eating disorders. It is easier to battle hunger than emotion.

LITTLE **BITES:** *Boys tend to perceive themselves as being overweight when they are actually 5 to 10 percent above average weight. Females tend to perceive themselves as being overweight when they are actually 13 to 15 percent below average weight.*[7]

BOYS AND EATING DISORDERS

Unlike girls, the majority of boys who develop eating disorders are actually somewhat overweight when the problem begins. As with girls, the desire to lose weight is often triggered by a comment from someone, or an insult or name-calling from peers. Studies indicate that boys tend to start dieting for three main reasons: to avoid being teased by others, to improve their sports' performance, and to avoid serious diseases like arteriosclerosis, heart disease, and cancer. More of them focus on taking the weight off through intense physical exercise than vomiting or refusing to eat. In fact, the term *exercise bulimia* is sometimes used to explain their behavior. Boys and young men also tend to abuse products that are designed to help them bulk up, or increase their muscle mass. Because they focus more on exercising than extreme food limiting, and because men tend to have more muscle mass to start with, it is harder to spot boys with eating disorders.

The **damage to boys' bones** from these conditions **is more severe** than that to girls' bones.

In fact, according to Dr. Arnold Andersen, director of the Eating Disorders Service at the University of Iowa's College of Medicine, the average anorexic male has the bones of an eighty-year-old man.[8]

The media has an affect on how males look at their appearance, too. Instead of a pressure to be slender, they are supposed to look lean, muscular, and powerful. They are supposed to have the broad shoulders, "six-pack abs," sculptured pecs, and narrow waist of Adonis. Those high standards are bound to make most young men feel inadequate and undersized. Soon, they find themselves suffering from a distorted body image known as body dysmorphia.

In some ways, it is the opposite of the female anorexic's body image; while girls cannot seem to get small enough, **boys cannot seem to get big enough.**

LITTLE **BITES:** *Boys involved in certain sports are at higher risk of developing eating disorders because their weight is crucial to their performance. These include jockeys, wrestlers, dancers, distance runners, and gymnasts.[9]*

83

ravages inside and out

DANNY'S STORY

Listening to Danny's story is not for the fainthearted. Now twenty-three and about to graduate from college, Danny is painfully honest about what he went through for many years.

Surprisingly, it started with surgery. When Danny was thirteen, he had his appendix out. Something went wrong during the operation, however, and he was put on complete bed rest for several months. That was not the only stress factor in his life at the time. "My parents were going through a divorce, my older brother was using drugs and running away, and my mom and I had moved six times in one year," he recalls. To cope with it all, Danny ate, and since he was in bed most of the time, he gained a lot of weight. "I started eighth grade weighing 200 pounds (91 kg). I was called names constantly," he admits.

One day, Danny's aunt patted him on the stomach and said, "You need to take care of this problem." She was right, thought Danny.

People will like me **if I am thin,** and then, if people like me, I can start **liking myself.**

Not long after that, Danny found the inspiration he needed in a most unlikely place. "Our health class was watching one of those educational videos they always show," he says. "It was about bulimia and showed these girls throwing up in jars. Everyone else was going 'ewwwwwww,' and it sounded like a great idea to me."

Danny ate his next meal and then purged right afterward. "It was like an alcoholic taking his first drink. The heavens opened up and I touched the stars. I knew that I had finally found what I needed to fix me."

Although he was hesitant to throw up too much at first, in a matter of months he "picked it up and ran with it." Soon, Danny could purge without sticking his finger down his throat. "I trained my muscles to be able to do it whenever I thought about it," he explains.

Danny's binging and purging continued for more than three years. His weight dropped from 200 pounds (91 kg) to an all-time low of 135 pounds (61 kg). At 5 foot 11 (180 cm), he was thin enough to worry his family. "My parents were very concerned and had me tested for everything," he says. "They checked to see if I had diabetes or if I was on drugs, but it was all clear."

Realization

Danny clearly remembers the moment that he realized something was really wrong with him. "I was coming out of the shower and had a towel wrapped around my waist," he recalls. "I looked in the mirror and for the first time, I saw myself as I really was, instead of focusing on the spots I wanted to improve. It was scary. I realized that

I was not doing this just to lose weight; I couldn't stop it.

At that point, I just wanted to die." He was sixteen years old.

Looking for something to help their son, Danny's parents sent him to stay with his twenty-year-old brother, Mike. "I was thrilled," says Danny. "I thought it was a great idea. While I was there, Mike happened to see me without my shirt and his jaw about hit the floor. He sat me down and asked if I was doing drugs. I said no, that was his thing, not mine. He asked if I was vomiting. I said no. And then," adds Danny, "I had one of those sudden moments of clarity. I hated my life, I hated myself, and I thought, what is the harm in finally just telling someone what I am doing? I told my brother I had been bulimic for a couple of years, and for the first time since it started, I cried. You just don't see that many happy people throwing up all day."

Mike immediately told his parents what was happening, and they were incredibly relieved to finally know what was wrong so that they could begin to address the problem. They found an outpatient counselor for Danny. He went one hour a week for a year, and, in his opinion, it was the equivalent of doing nothing at all. "It was worthless for me because I was too deep into it," he explains. "It was too easy to just lie to the counselor." He got a brief break when he found a girlfriend. "I decided I'd just quit for her," he admits, and for an entire month, Danny stopped vomiting. "I couldn't believe I could do that!" When they broke up, however, Danny's bulimia returned, and he said it was twice as bad as it was before.

"I was completely suicidal," he said. "I would dig holes in the ground and vomit, and I would binge and purge in public.

I guess the **lows of my dignity** knew no bounds at that point."

87

Hitting Bottom

Things just continued to get worse. The night after Danny's junior prom, he had a big argument with his mom and stepfather. He took off in the car and binged on a "mountain" of cinnamon rolls, slowing down long enough to purge along the way. "I came home, sat down, and said, I need to go to treatment," says Danny. "My mom just said, 'Thank God.' I didn't want to go to a hospital where they locked you in your room and monitored you. It was really hard to find a place that would take guys, too." Danny's family found an inpatient institution in their state. "The original plan was to be there for forty-two days as an inpatient and thirty days in transition," he explains. "However, when we had Family Week, that all changed." The week where all the family members gather to discuss the issues underlying an eating disorder did not go well. In fact, it was a bit of a disaster. All of the family's personal issues and problems came to the surface, and when it was over, the institute recommended that Danny spend his entire senior year with them instead of just forty-two days.

"I stopped throwing up from the first day I walked in there," says Danny. "I had made two promises to myself. The first one was to do whatever they told me to do. The second was that if this didn't work, I was going to kill myself."

Fortunately, the treatment worked. Danny learned a lot while he was there, including gaining some insight into how women dealt with eating disorders. "Going to group therapy with twenty or thirty women ruined the male chauvinist in me for life," he says ruefully. "Now I know these girls have real feelings!"

At the end of Danny's senior year, he went straight to college. Although he had a lot of culture shock to deal with, he continued to improve. He spent some time in the Marines and was even stationed in Iraq for a period of time. Today, he considers himself a healthy, happy human being who has completely recovered from his bulimia. He credits one person with that recovery— himself. "I have a great support system," he says, "but the only person who really made a difference was me. An eating disorder is not about how you look or how much you weigh. It's about how you feel about yourself. The disorder is comfortable and familiar and keeps you from taking risks. It reflects the hate that you are feeling toward yourself, and it gets tiring to feel that way. You simply have to make a decision or choice to do something different. I did."[10]

W E I G H T Y   W O R D S

"All of the people who suffer from eating disorders need supportive parents who consciously and unconsciously relay the message that they are beautiful just the way they are."

~ *Dr. Kathryn Zerbe, author of* The Body Betrayed[11]

---

ravages inside and out ►

CHAPTER MENU

In this chapter you will:

- ❧ *Discover how Rachel and Laura survived their eating disorders*
- ❧ *Learn about different kinds of therapy used to treat eating disorders*
- ❧ *Take a look inside some eating disorder clinics*
- ❧ *Find out about the Internet mecca for victims of eating disorders*

CHAPTER FOUR

SEEKING SUSTENANCE: THE SEARCH FOR HOPE

RACHEL'S STORY By the time she was sixteen, Rachel knew she had a problem. She had been excessively restricting her food intake for more than six months. "It all began with just wanting to go on a diet and lose some weight," explains Rachel.

"I was feeling really **insecure,** and dieting was the only way I knew to **feel better," about myself** that I could feel **good about."**

Rachel was successful at losing weight. Too successful. Eventually, her friends started to worry about her. "They said they could barely recognize me. I couldn't understand that because I really had no perception of how I looked. My image never changed or looked thinner to me. I thought that the scales were wrong." At 5 foot 4 (163 cm), Rachel's weight was down to 100 lbs (45 kg). Her mother finally suggested that they see a psychologist. "I went one to two times a week for four or five months," says Rachel. "He told me I either had to improve or go to the hospital." Rachel began to eat more for several weeks, but she was also purging eight to ten times a day.

By the end of that summer, Rachel was in big trouble. A friend had discovered her daily vomiting and had told Rachel's mother. The psychologist decided

more intensive treatment was needed and so, just
before she was to begin her senior year of high school,
Rachel was put into outpatient care at an institution.
She went there from 8:00 A.M. to 3:00 P.M. for weeks. "I
was just going through the motions so I could return to
school," she admits now. She was seeing a psychiatrist,
a psychologist, and a nutritionist but the restricting,
purging, and laxative use was only getting worse.

Many different kinds of health care professionals can be
involved in an eating disorder patient's treatment.

Turning Point

Rachel was in and out of the outpatient program for weeks. Then one day, she learned something important. "I suddenly realized that this thing was a lot bigger than me. It was time to do something else." This time around, Rachel went to the institution as an inpatient. For three weeks, she was there 24/7. "We were up at 5:00 A.M. and weighed blindly," she recalls. "They took our vitals, and then we went back to sleep. After breakfast, I met with my therapist and psychologist three times a week, and the rest of the time was in group therapy. From the time I woke up in the morning until I went to sleep at night, all I did was talk," she explains. "I was forced to confront deeper issues. I'd already dealt with all of the surface stuff. If you didn't talk in group therapy, your privileges were taken away. I really wanted to do well and to succeed," she adds.

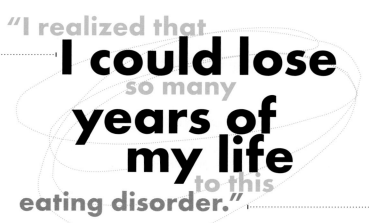

"I realized that **I could lose** so many **years of my life** to this **eating disorder.**"

"The longer you have it, the harder it is to get rid of it. People turn away from you and you know you are failing them and failing yourself. I saw others who had no hope left at all. The eating disorder had become their whole lives." Seeing the devastation that eating disorders can bring to people's lives inspired Rachel to work hard in treatment.

Today, **she has recovered** from her disorder **and is headed for college to get a degree** in marketing or education.

Rachel's experience inspired her family to create A Chance to Heal, a nonprofit organization that provides financial assistance to those who can't afford treatment for eating disorders. "I started A Chance to Heal with my mother because I had watched as our insurance ran out and she had to pay for my treatment out of her own pocket," says Rachel. "I felt so grateful, yet also so guilty. Why was I allowed to recover, when others could not?" Thanks to hard work and corporate and individual donors, Rachel has raised more than $50,000 so far.[1]

seeking sustenance: the search for hope

THE WIDE WORLD OF TREATMENT

There are many theories and philosophies on the best way to treat anorexia and bulimia. Some people put the care of the physical body first, while others focus on the emotional elements. Regardless of where they start, however, most treatment involves a team of players that includes a psychiatrist and psychologist (to deal with the mental and emotional aspects of the disease), a dietary professional or nutritionist (to work on weight restoration), a medical doctor (to deal with medical complications), and sometimes a **gastroenterologist** (to deal with specific digestive conditions). Occasionally, the team also includes a social worker and a nurse. Whoever is on the team, the goals are almost always the same: normalizing weight, resolving underlying psychological issues, and establishing long-lasting healthy eating habits.

WEIGHTY WORDS

"Eating disorders are not about weight and food, though their symptoms would have everyone 'on the outside' fooled into thinking so. These illnesses are about an inability to cope with life and stress; they are about low self-esteem and feeling out of control; and they are an internal power struggle for survival."

~ Amy Medina[2]

OUTPATIENT OR INPATIENT?

Management of eating disorders can be done on an outpatient or an inpatient basis, depending on the severity of the condition.

Outpatient care usually means regular meetings with therapists and perhaps family therapy, group therapy, or both. Inpatient care means everything from around-the-clock monitoring to tube feeding and total bed rest.

WEIGHTY WORDS

"I ended up with no friends and no life, locked behind closed doors in a psychiatric ward. All my friends had gone on to college or had married, and I had none of those things. Eventually, eating disorders consume your whole life. They don't lead to happiness! They take everything away."[3]

PSYCHOTHERAPY

The types of therapy used in these clinics and institutions differ and often overlap. Assuming the patient is physically capable of getting therapy, doctors usually focus on helping the patient admit to and face the underlying issues contributing to the eating disorder. They will ask a lot of questions:

✳ **Do you feel overly pressured?**

✳ **Do you find food a way to keep some element of control in your life?**

✳ **Do you have problems communicating with your parents (more than the usual, that is)?**

✳ **Have you been physically or sexually abused?**

✳ **How do you cope with stress?**

✳ **What do you believe triggered your eating disorder?**

✳ **How do you feel when you're restricting, binging, or compulsively exercising?**

✳ **What do you see when you look in the mirror?**

✳ **Most important, do you want to survive this?**

These aren't questions that most people want to answer, but many experts truly believe that recognizing and accepting the issues has to come before healing can begin. If a patient is not willing to try and does not want to improve, therapy rarely makes a difference.

WEIGHTY WORDS

"I am a firm believer there is life after an eating disorder. Some do get completely cured. Treatment is really important. It can make the difference between a chronic case and one that is cured."

~ Mae Sokol, MD[4]

CHALLENGING DISTORTED PERCEPTIONS

Distorted perceptions of how you look, how you feel about food, and the way you do or do not eat will all be challenged in treatment. For many people with eating disorders, these distortions provide a sense of safety and control ("I do not know how much sugar I can eat, so I will just never eat any at all"). They can also serve as part of a patient's identity ("I am known for skipping breakfast and lunch on most days"). They even help explain their odd behavior to others ("You know I can't eat that because I am allergic to nuts/tomatoes/milk"). Therapists will usually point out that behaviors are always choices and that the ones the patient has been making are not only wrong, but dangerous. Patients are shown how to replace those dangerous behaviors with safe ones. Patients find out more about themselves than they ever knew before. Hopefully, in doing so, they will also find the key to what is happening so they can begin the journey to recovery.

LITTLE **BITES:** *In sorority houses and cafeterias across the country, normal eating is no longer healthy eating. Students report being made to feel like "gluttons" when they eat meals in front of peers who pride themselves on "meals" of water or Diet Coke.[5]*

LITTLE **BITES:** *In 1995, a psychological study found that three minutes of looking at a fashion magazine caused 70 percent of women to feel depressed, guilty, and shameful.[6]*

A LOOK INSIDE SOME PROGRAMS

THE MANDOMETER CLINIC

Dr. Cecelia Burgh's basic philosophy is to treat the physical symptoms of eating disorders rather than the psychological aspects. "The psychological symptoms go away as normal eating returns," she says. She does it with a device known as the Mandometer. "Mando is the name of the device we use," she adds. "It means 'I eat.' It works like a crutch for a broken leg." Burgh feels that most eating disorder patients have lost the ability to recognize what a normal serving of food is and how to judge when they are full. During treatment, servings of food are attached to a scale so that serving size is controlled. Patients are shown the rate at which they are eating and the rate at which they should be eating to be within normal parameters. Patients are asked to rate their **satiety** or fullness and compare it to normal levels. All of this helps them relearn what is normal. After eating, patients are taken to a warm room where they can relax. "They love these rooms," explains Dr. Bergh. "Usually they are freezing. This helps to reduce anxiety and stress and stop panic attacks." Often patients will fall asleep while in these rooms.

seeking sustenance: the search for hope

Cured?

Along with the controlled eating and the warm rooms, the clinic provides case managers who talk, guide, and coach the patients from day one through remission.

The average length of stay for patients is fifteen months.

The Mandometer Clinic has very strict requirements for considering someone officially cured. Patients must show that they have normal eating behaviors, body weight, and blood tests, and a normal psychiatric profile. You must return to school or work and, if you were bulimic, you must be free of binging and purging for at least three months. According to studies done at the clinic, 70 percent of their patients meet these criteria and maintain this status for several years.[7]

A patient uses a Mandometer while eating a meal.

REMUDA RANCH
TREATMENT CENTER

Remuda Ranch is located in Arizona about 45 miles (72 km) northwest of Phoenix. It is the nation's largest treatment center for anorexia, bulimia, and related eating disorders. Since opening in 1990, it has treated more than six thousand children, teens, and women. The founder of Remuda is a man named Ward Keller. He knows on a personal level what eating disorders can do to a family. His ten-year-old daughter developed anorexia after her friend was killed in a car accident. She stopped eating, and when her parents took her to the doctor, medical tests showed nothing. Keller was a successful businessman, and he was sure he could get his daughter to eat. He didn't see any point in therapy because he believed that was only for the weak. He was wrong. It didn't work. Finally, a therapist told Keller that he must prove to his daughter how important she was to him. To do so, he bought Remuda Ranch as a place for her recovery. He established the ranch on Christian principles. Their mission statement is "to help individuals suffering from eating disorders with programs that are biblically based and scientifically valid."

The Remuda Program

The director of psychological services at the ranch is Dr. David Wall. He says that many of the patients they see there are running from family system issues. "We all need to feel that we are special and irreplaceable.

Remuda Ranch offers programs for adults, teenagers, and younger children.

Eating disorders are like a remote control," he says. "You push the buttons to get your parents to stop smoking or fighting and pay attention to you instead. They start to listen and focus on you. If they lose their eating disorder, what will happen then?"

Remuda focuses on four different aspects of a person: genetic (the biological factors of eating disorders), psychological (feeling unique and loved), social (media and the culture's bias against people with weight issues), and spiritual (the role of God). It offers programs for adults, adolescents, and children. These programs include individual and group therapy, nutrition classes, daily chapel, and family visits. In addition to these more traditional offerings, they also have equine (horse) therapy; a challenge course; art, music, movement, and creative writing therapy; and recreational activities.[8]

seeking sustenance: the search for hope

FOUNDING THE BELLA VITA

The Bella Vita is located in Pasadena, California. Dr. Patricia Pitts is the executive director and a clinical psychologist who knows what it is like to deal with anorexia.

The year before starting junior high is often full of fear and worry about the future. For Patricia, it was also filled with worry about her weight. At 5 foot 6 (168 cm), she weighed 109 pounds (49 kg) but felt that was too much. She began to restrict what she ate, and it wasn't long before she was down to 70 pounds (32 kg). "I became my own cage," she admits. "No one could come in, and I could not get out."

When her parents took her to the doctor, he just told her to start eating. "He was a jerk," she recalls with a frown. By ninth grade, she was eating, but was also binging and purging. That came to a stop in eleventh grade when she began dating her high school sweetheart. "I did not have an eating disorder for that entire year," she says. "Having that relationship took away the focus on food and off my inner self." When they broke up the following year, her eating disorder returned.

Patricia finally found the help she needed. "It was the love and care of my sister Susan that finally broke through and showed me I was out of control," she says. After she recovered, she went on to do what others have done: share the hope. She became a psychologist who specializes in working with young people who have eating disorders. In 1985, she established The Bella Vita, a program that offers inpatient and outpatient care.

A nutritionist works with a patient to develop the patient's awareness of normal food portions.

The Program

The Bella Vita outpatient program is designed so that the patient can still attend school or go to work and is usually for people who either have less severe problems or are already recovering from their disorders. The longer hospitalization program is for those who are having more problems and need a structured environment.

Daily schedules at The Bella Vita often include individual therapy, group therapy, sessions on body image, goal setting and relapse prevention, art therapy, guided imagery, family consultations, and individualized meal plans. Other activities offered are Family Day and Family Night, restaurant outings, grocery shopping, potlucks, yoga, and aromatherapy.[9]

WEIGHTY WORDS

"When People *magazine ran a story on stars who had lost 20 to 30 pounds [9 to 14 kg], we immediately saw a drastic increase in the number of patients at Bella Vita."*

~Dr. Patricia Pitts, executive director of the Bella Vita Program[10]

---

seeking sustenance: the search for hope

WEIGHTY WORDS

"Probably the most important turning point in my recovery was my decision to become an active participant in the process. From then on, I was no longer a passive bystander; I was working to get well and to improve my life. Of course, I still had bad days. In time, the good days outnumbered the bad. Through many years of failed treatment, I learned that in order to get well, I had to want recovery. Nobody could climb inside my head and make that change for me."[11]

CHOOSING A TREATMENT OPTION

Deciding what kind of therapy is best for someone with an eating disorder is terribly challenging. "There is not one single effective therapy," says Dr. Kathryn Zerbe, author of *The Body Betrayed: Women, Eating Disorders and Treatment.* "Treatment must be individualized." One simple step that she recommends for families is to reinstate the old-fashioned tradition of the family eating together at the table. "The family meal is getting more nonexistent," she explains. "Kids eat alone, there is no discussion of the day and no actual human contact. There is physical and emotional nurturance in sharing a meal," she adds. "It helps to metabolize the day."[12]

WEIGHTY WORDS

"Waiting for the breakfast to arrive was so strange, having spent the last five years constantly on a diet. I didn't know how food tasted anymore. Amidst all the terror of being in this institution, there was also a weird feeling of safety, like a young child when he is fed in a high chair. Now, in the hospital, I was being forced to eat. This was a relief because, like all anorexics, I had always felt hungry. For years, day and night, I desperately wanted to eat. It was only the voice that stopped me from eating, even though my whole adult life I was starving. The voice had for years been a central point of my life and the only way to get the voice to love me was not to eat. Now, with the nurses threatening me with a drip feed, the voice was overruled and had no choice but to allow the food being given by the hospital."[13]

seeking sustenance: the search for hope

IN THE NEWS:
THE ANOREXIC VALEDICTORIAN

Karen Scherr knows that getting treatment is a priority for someone suffering from an eating disorder—even if it means missing out on something you've worked hard for and looked forward to for a long time.

For all of her four years at Kingwood High School in Houston, Texas, Karen was at the top of her class. She also had anorexia. Because she took the time to go to a treatment facility and get the help she needed, she was told that she was not qualified to win the title of valedictorian. Her grades were the highest in the class, but all candidates for the coveted title had to be enrolled in classes on the twentieth day of their junior year. This requirement was meant to keep other students from transferring to Kingswood late in their high school careers and taking one of the prized academic honors.

Karen had been in the same school system since kindergarten, but on that special day she was somewhere else—in an institution getting lifesaving help. She missed the first six weeks of her junior year and was disqualified.

"I was disappointed," admits Scherr. "I'd hoped the rule would not have to be enforced." So did her classmates. There were pleas and petitions asking for her to get the title, but the school refused.

Although she wasn't happy with the decision, Scherr

says she would not change a thing if she could do it all over again. Treatment was the priority. "That was the best decision. I don't regret it at all," she says. "It was a choice made with input from my parents and doctors. I'm okay with it."

Kingwood offered Scherr the title of Honorary Valedictorian and, after thinking about it, she accepted. Despite her disappointment in not being given the title of valedictorian, Scherr's self-esteem is intact. And that, she says, is "more important than any achievement or any title you could ever get. I'm thankful I've learned that at this point in my life, at 18 years old."[14]

WEIGHTY WORDS

"Often what happens when you see anorexics in a group is that they start to compete with each other. They are vying to be the best anorexic ever. But the best anorexics are dead."

~ Vivian Hanson Meehan, president of the National Association of Anorexia and Associated Disorders[15]

LAURA'S STORY

"Looking back, I can see that the seeds for my eating disorder were planted at puberty," says Laura. "It wasn't full-blown until early college, though."

In Laura's teen years, she dieted now and then and found that walking also helped her lose pounds. She kept it up, and by the time she entered college, she was working her way into a real problem. "It lasted for nine months," she recalls, "and I finally got down to 85 pounds (39 kg)

People with eating disorders may spend a lot of time reading food labels in an attempt to avoid eating "bad" foods.

at 5 feet 4 inches (163 cm). I had no periods and was restricting the number of calories I ate each day." As the pounds came off, however, Laura said that her reflection never changed. "You just cannot reconcile what you are doing and what you see in the mirror."

Although she knew she was in trouble, it was not until she came home for summer vacation that it really became obvious. "I saw how rigid I was about what I could and could not eat," she says, "and I just could not imagine doing this for years. I was so aware of the paranoia that went with this condition. I knew that food labels were lying to me because the anorexic mind translates everything into a threat. I knew I would have to gain weight if I was ever going to have my freedom again."

Laura was wise. She immediately joined a support group at college and then began seeing a therapist for a year. Soon she had learned to fill up her life with things, rather than obsessing about food. By the end of her college years, she had recovered.

Today, Laura is Dr. Laura Ellick and she has taken her experience and turned it into a life's mission. As a psychologist, she specializes in helping teens with eating disorders. "Recovery is certainly possible, and it doesn't have to mean getting fat," she reassures her patients. "You can have freedom from this obsession. I did it!"[16]

LITTLE **BITES:** *A 2005 nationwide poll showed that 96 percent of Americans believe eating disorders are serious illnesses. Of those, 81 percent thought they could be successfully treated.[17]*

seeking sustenance: the search for hope

113

CHAPTER MENU

In this chapter you will:

- ❖ *Read the story of a mother's search for help for her daughter*
- ❖ *Look at how you can help and support a friend with anorexia or bulimia*
- ❖ *Read the story of Sandy's search for help and hope in her life*

CHAPTER FIVE

WHAT CAN I DO?

DAWN AND AMANDA'S STORY Dawn figured that she had to be the worst mother in the world. "My daughter was being tortured and teased, and I didn't even know it," she says. "Parenting doesn't come with an instruction book, so I knew I could either sit around and feel guilty or do something to help Amanda."

Amanda had grown up with an older sister who was 5 foot 9 (175 cm) and a homecoming queen and an older brother who was a whiz on the football field. All she heard was that she was built like her daddy, who was stocky. She struggled with her weight from childhood. Hoping that exercise would help her lose weight, she joined the elementary school swim team. At the age of seven, she won her first swim meet. As she proudly walked up to get her trophy, a young boy said, "Wow, I didn't know that Shamu was in the pool today." Amanda's mother, Dawn, didn't hear it, but Amanda did.

The following year, in second grade, Amanda joined the school choir. After a solo performance for the PTA, a classmate told her, "You don't need a choir robe. You need a tent!"

Amanda never swam or sang again.

By the time she got to high school, she had started running to lose weight. She ran two, three, four, even five miles a day. The pounds melted off—and kept right on melting. "At first, we all encouraged her and told her how terrific and great she was doing," states Dawn. That did not last long. Amanda had been diagnosed with attention deficit disorder (ADD), and at a meeting, a teacher asked Dawn what she was going to do about her daughter's eating disorder. "What disorder?" was Dawn's response. The teacher confided that her own daughter was in the hospital, dying from heart failure brought on by anorexia, and she recognized the signs in Amanda.

During her senior year in high school, Amanda spent her Christmas vacation with her father and older brother. Amanda's brother confronted Dawn during that time.

"What are you going to do about Amanda?" he demanded. To Dawn's horror, he told her that while Amanda was visiting, he had seen her throwing up at least three separate times. Dawn went to her daughter and began asking questions. "With crystal clear blue eyes like a pool, she looked right at me and admitted it all," recalls Dawn. "She was vomiting almost ten times a day, as well as taking laxatives and diuretics. She had no regrets whatsoever. It was absolutely heartbreaking."

Some anorexics run for miles every day to maintain their feeling of control over their weight.

Getting Help

For the next three months, Dawn searched for a therapist who specialized in eating disorders. "One doctor just gave Amanda some sleeping pills," she says bitterly, "and they almost killed her." Finally, they were forced to look out of state for help. The cost was astronomical, and their insurance would not cover it. Amanda was sent to a clinic in Florida. It was her first time away from home, and she was there for forty-five days. "I got a call from the clinic saying that she was being 'noncompliant,' " says Dawn. Amanda came back home, finished high school, and immediately got married. She had two children, both born prematurely because of complications.

Six months later, Amanda's eating disorder intensified. She had severely restricted her intake of calories. She was also taking laxatives and walking a couple of miles daily. She dropped to 90 pounds (41 kg). Her life was in danger. "That is when I found Remuda Ranch," says Dawn. It is one of the country's oldest established eating disorders institutes. Amanda was there for sixty days in intensive care, and it saved her life. "Remuda has a biblically based doctrine," explains Dawn, "and combines it with activities like equine therapy, where the girls get to groom and ride horses, as well as participate in challenge courses. There is no time to sit and feel sorry for yourself there."

Equine therapy is part of the treatment program at Remuda Ranch and other facilities that deal with eating disorders or other psychological illnesses.

Helping Others

Dawn uses her experience with Amanda to help others struggling with eating disorders. She started Lifelines Foundation for Eating Disorders six years ago. She and her husband, shocked at the lack of educational materials for schools about eating disorders, designed a complete packet, including posters, handouts, and booklets. Amanda wrote the introduction. Thanks to $120,000 worth of grants, they were able to print thousands of these educational packets—which are now sitting in a warehouse waiting for the funds to distribute them. "I travel, speak, and hand out materials as much as I can," says Dawn. "Helping people with eating disorders means empowerment.

You have to get to **the core** of the eating issue. Find out **what took away** their feelings **of control.**

Family therapy is absolutely essential," she adds. "They will need help and support down the road."[1]

120

LITTLE **BITES:** *Eighty percent of American women polled stated that they were dissatisfied with their overall appearance.*[2]

IF YOU NEED HELP

No matter where you live, someone nearby is suffering from an eating disorder. It might be the person sitting next to you in algebra class. It might be your neighbor's nephew. It might be your co-worker's daughter. It could even be someone closer, like your cousin or your best friend. It might even be you.

If you suspect you might have an eating disorder, you should find a counselor or other trusted adult to talk with right away.

what can I do?

Then do some research. Go to the library and check out a few books. Go online and read some of the information you find there. Do you see your reflection in the words you read? If so, ask yourself some important questions:

DO YOU HAVE A PROBLEM?

✳ How much time do you spend thinking about your weight?

✳ How much time do you spend thinking about what you eat?

✳ Have you recently lost a great deal of weight?

✳ Have people made comments to you about your weight?

✳ Do you always feel cold?

✳ Are your periods regular?

✳ Do you ever feel out of control when you are eating?

✳ Are you vomiting?

✳ Do you use laxatives, diuretics, or herbs to help you lose weight?

✳ How often do you weigh yourself?

✳ How much time per day do you spend exercising?

✳ Does your weight interfere with your daily life in any way?

✳ How do you feel about food?

✳ What thoughts do you have when you look at yourself in the mirror?

Analyze your answers. Take what you have learned and apply it to your responses. What do those answers tell you?

If you are concerned, don't wait another moment. Tell someone.

Get help immediately before things get worse. Your life is the most important thing there is, and you need to make sure it is safe.

What else can you do? Here are a few suggestions:

TAKE CARE OF YOURSELF

* Talk to someone you trust about what you are experiencing.
* Set positive goals for yourself daily.
* Focus on the blessings in your life.
* Take time to pamper yourself.
* Appreciate your accomplishments.
* Keep a journal of your feelings.
* Avoid using the scales.

what can I do?

IF SOMEONE ELSE NEEDS HELP

As you read the information in this book, did you begin thinking of someone you know? If the person you are wondering about is someone you can talk to directly, do it carefully. Encourage the person to go straight to his parents and let them know what is happening. If he refuses, let him know that you will do so instead. Going behind his back will only make him feel as if he has been betrayed. If it is an adult, urge the person to seek professional help from one of the many local, national, or online organizations that exist.

The point of your message is clear: You care and want to help.

Be patient and kind. Be compassionate. Listen and do not get angry or fight with the person. Do not assume the role of therapist either. You are simply someone who cares enough to speak up.

SANDY'S STORY

Although eating disorders often strike young women, it can hit at other ages as well. Just ask Sandy. Her early life was not easy or smooth. She was sexually and physically abused as a child. She grew up to abuse drugs, alcohol, and sex in return. She joined the Air Force and eventually met a man named Scott. After a few months, they were married. "I was sure he could fix me," explains Sandy, "because he didn't know the real me—the bad person inside."

For the first time, while in her early 30s, Sandy found another way to fill up the emptiness inside of her. "It felt good to not eat," she says, "and in two months, I had lost 30 pounds." At almost 5 feet 5 inches (165 cm), Sandy was underweight at just 99 pounds (45 kg).

It was not long before Sandy got pregnant, and she had to gain weight to maintain the pregnancy. As soon as the baby was born, she returned to not eating and purging when she did eat. Soon, she had another child and the family moved. "My husband was gone for two months for Air Force training and I was at home with a newborn and a toddler," recalls Sandy. "I knew I needed help. I would sit at the kitchen table and eat, knowing I was just going to go in and throw it up a few minutes later."

"Lately, I had been throwing up blood, and I was worried."

Sandy then had what she thinks was a miracle occur. She was looking through a woman's magazine and happened to spot an ad for Remuda Ranch. It was the first ad they had placed in a publication.

Not Alone

"I was floored by the knowledge that there were enough women out there to have a hospital just for them," says Sandy. She picked up the phone to call, and when someone answered, she hung up—then called back again. Twelve days later, she was at the ranch. She told family and friends that she had gone to a special clinic that treated PMS (premenstrual syndrome). "I stayed there for seventy-four days, and it was horrible at first," she admits. "I hadn't connected my past with the eating issues yet. I had to relive the abuse. Putting myself back in that place and discussing it, plus eating and not vomiting, was so hard."

Sandy found comfort and guidance in an unexpected place. "I was sitting at Remuda and flipping through a Bible in an attempt to look spiritual when a verse popped up about ignoring the past, and I began crying," she describes.

"Once I had hope, I was more open to the pain."

It has been a long, difficult trip for Sandy. Her husband stood by her throughout it all, but, as she put it, "It was like being chained to a roller coaster. Scott was a fighter pilot, and he just did not understand what I was going through. He is not emotionally accessible, but we are still together after twenty-four years."

Sandy went back into the hospital two more times. Finally, she began to recover, and in the process, she realized that a lot of her life was wrapped up in Remuda. So much so, in fact, that she did not want to let it go. In 1999, she became the executive director there, and today, she does a lot of public speaking at schools, hospitals, and women's groups on the organization's behalf while working on her master's degree in counseling. In 1999, she also published *Soul Hunger*, a reference for others who, like her, had to escape from the pervasive power of an eating disorder.[3]

what can I do?

127

A FEW LAST CRUMBS

In 1996, a lovely young college student named Elisa Ruth McCall died at the age of twenty.

Like too many others, she had **anorexia so severe** that **it killed her.**

Her parents have taken her journals and letters and made them part of the Elisa Ruth McCall Memorial Endowment Fund at Southern Methodist University. Her writings are posted online for others to read and hopefully gain support, education, and understanding. On the next page is a letter that truly gives you insight into the thoughts and mind of someone going through this terrible condition. Read it carefully. Think about it. Don't let it happen to someone you care about. Don't let it happen to you. There are no do-overs in life—no second chances to go back and do things differently. The time is now. The choice is yours. Speak up and speak out.

Dear Elisa,

You've taken everything I say so seriously. From the first time I spoke to you when you weighed 107 lbs. "You're gonna be a fat girl and you're only 13! Better watch it!" I labeled food good and bad. I've told you you're fat and worthless. I've told you no guy would ever like you because you're fat. I've told you you're a failure and a disappointment to your parents. I've told you it's amazing you have friends and unbelievable anyone could care for such a sick slob. I've said the most terrible things anyone has ever said to you and you've listened as if I were God. You've taken it all to heart and let it shape and mold you. I control your life. In order to get rid of me you must stop listening to my terrible voice. My advice has gotten you nowhere. You need to realize you have given me complete control and then you need to take back what is rightfully yours. You must stop feeling through me and face the intensity of those feelings alone. You must stop using me for protection and excuses.

In order to get rid of me, you must stand up for yourself and believe in yourself. You must learn to love yourself and stop waiting for my acceptance... for I will never approve. It is possible for you to exist without me. You must find your own identity and become your own person.

Signed,
Your Eating Disorder[4]

GLOSSARY

amenorrhea a temporary cessation of regular monthly menstrual periods

anorexia a psychological condition where the person begins to purposely starve himself or herself; the word means "without appetite"

anorexia athletica the term used to describe compulsive or addictive exercise

binge to do something, such as eating, in a larger than usual amount, often quite quickly

bulimia a psychological condition where the person purposely binges and purges; the word means "appetite of an ox"

dehydration a loss of fluids

diuretics medications that remove extra fluids from the body

electrolytes ions such as sodium, potassium, or chloride that cells need in order to regulate the electric charge within the body

endorphins hormones found in the brain that reduce the feeling of pain and affect the emotions

estrogen one of the female hormones that controls the development of the reproductive organs and secondary sex characteristics

gastroenterologist a physician that specializes in treating digestive disorders

hyperventilate to breathe too rapidly and deeply, usually due to stress or anxiety

ipecac a medical preparation that induces vomiting

lanugo a soft coating of hair

laxatives a medical preparation that is used to stimulate bowel movements

menstrual related to menstruation

neurotransmitters molecules that work as messengers between brain functions

osteoporosis a medical condition in which the bones do not get enough calcium and become brittle and easy to fracture

purge to get rid of forcibly, in the case of bulimia, through vomiting, medication, or exercise

satiety the sensation of fullness or beyond; comfortably satisfied

serotonin a neurotransmitter that affects appetite, mood, and other brain functions

testosterone the male hormone responsible for the development and growth of reproductive organs and secondary sexual characteristics

TO FIND OUT MORE

BOOKS

Fairburn, Christopher G. *Overcoming Binge Eating.* New York: Guilford Press, 1995.

Heaton, Jeanne Albranda, and Claudia J. Strauss. *Talking to Eating Disorders: Simple Ways to Support Someone with Anorexia, Bulimia, Binge Eating or Body Image Issues.* New York: New American Library, 2005.

Hendricks, Jennifer. *Slim to None: A Journey through the Wasteland of Anorexia Treatment.* New York: McGraw-Hill, 2003.

Lerner, Betsy. *Food and Loathing: A Life Measured Out in Calories.* New York: Simon and Schuster, 2003.

Levenkron, Steven. *Anatomy of Anorexia.* New York: W. W. Norton and Company, 2001.

Levenkron, Steven. *The Best Little Girl in the World.* New York: Warner Books, 1997.

Lucas, Alexander R. *Demystifying Anorexia: An Optimistic Guide to Understanding and Healing.* New York: Oxford University Press, 2004.

Maisel, Richard, David Epston, and Ali Borden. *Biting the Hand That Starves You: Inspiring Resistance to Anorexia and Bulimia.* New York: W. W. Norton and Company, 2004.

Schaefer, Jenni, and Thom Rutledge. *Life without ED: How One Woman Declared Independence from her Eating Disorder and How You Can Too.* New York: McGraw-Hill, 2004.

ONLINE SITES AND ORGANIZATIONS

ACADEMY FOR EATING DISORDERS (EAD)
6728 Old McLean Village Drive
McClean, VA 22101
703-556-9222
www.acadeatdis.org

AMERICAN ANOREXIA/BULIMIA ASSOCIATION, INC. (AABA)
165 East 46th Street, Suite 1108
New York, NY 10036
212-575-6200
http://members.aol.com/amaanbu

ANOREXIA NERVOSA AND RELATED EATING DISORDERS (ANRED)
PO Box 5102
Eugene, OR 97405
541-344-1144
www.anred.com

BULIMIA ANOREXIA SELF HELP INC. (BASH)
6125 Clayton Avenue, Suite 215
St. Louis, MO 63139
314-567-4080

CENTER FOR THE STUDY OF ANOREXIA AND BULIMIA
1841 Broadway, 4th Floor
New York, NY 63139
212-333-3444

A CHANCE TO HEAL
1457 Noble Road
Rydal, PA 19046
215-885-2420
info@achancetoheal.org

EATING ADDICTIONS ANONYMOUS
PO Box 8151
Silver Spring, MD 20907
202-882-6528

EATING DISORDERS ANONYMOUS
18233 North 16th Way
Phoenix, AZ 85022
602-788-4990

EATING DISORDERS AWARENESS AND PREVENTION INC. (EDAP)
National Eating Disorders Association (NEDA)
603 Stewart Street, Suite 803
Seattle, WA 98101
206-382-3587
http://members.aol.com/edapinc
www.nationaleatingdisorders.org

EATING DISORDERS COALITION FOR RESEARCH, POLICY AND ACTION
611 Pennsylvania Avenue
SE,Suite 423
Washington, DC 20003
202-543-9570
www.eatingdisorderscoalition.org

THE ELISA PROJECT
5950 Berkshire Lane, #1410
Dallas, TX 75225
214-369-5222

HARVARD EATING DISORDERS CENTER
Massachusetts General Hospital
WACC-7275
15 Parkman Street
Boston, MA 02114
617-236-7766
www.hedc.org

INTERNATIONAL ASSOCIATION OF EATING DISORDERS PROFESSIONALS (IAEDP)
PO Box 1295
Pekin, IL 61555
800-800-8126

NATIONAL ANOREXIA AID SOCIETY (NAAS)
Harding Hospital
1925 East Dublin Granville Road
Columbus, OH 43229
614-436-1112

NATIONAL ASSOCIATION OF ANOREXIA NERVOSA AND ASSOCIATED DISORDERS (ANAD)
PO Box 7
Highland Park, IL 60035
847-831-3438
http://members.aol.com/anad20/index.html

NATIONAL EATING DISORDERS SCREENING PROGRAM (NEDSP)
National Mental Health Illness Screening Project, Inc.
One Washington Street
Suite 304
Wellesley Hills, WA 02481
781-239-0071

IN CANADA

BULIMIA ANOREXIA NERVOSA ASSOCIATION (BANA)
300 Cabana Road E
Windsor, ON N9G 1A3
519-969-2112
www.bana.ca

**EATING DISORDERS
RESOURCE CENTRE OF
BRITISH COLUMBIA**
4500 Oak Street
Room E200 Mailbox 134
Vancouver, BC V6H 3N1
604-875-2084

**NATIONAL EATING DISORDER
INFORMATION CENTRE
(NEDIC)**
200 Elizabeth Street
Toronto, ON M5G 2C4
416-340-4736
www.medic.ca

WHERE TO CALL FOR HELP

These places want to help you, so reach out and talk to them.

**ANOREXIA NERVOSA AND
ASSOCIATED DISORDERS**
847-831-3438

**BULIMIA AND SELF-HELP
HOTLINE**
314-588-1683

**NATIONAL ADOLESCENT
SUICIDE HOTLINE**
800-621-4000

**NATIONAL EATING
DISORDERS ASSOC.**
800-931-2237

**NATIONAL EATING
DISORDER REFERRAL AND
INFORMATION CENTER**
858-481-1515

**THE NATIONAL MENTAL
HEALTH ASSOC.
INFORMATION CENTER**
800-969-NMHA
(800-969-6642)

NATIONAL SUICIDE HOTLINE
800-SUICIDE
(800-784-2433)

OVEREATER'S ANONYMOUS
505-891-4320

RADER PROGRAMS
800-841-1515

RENFREW CENTER
800-RENFREW
(800-736-3739)

THERAPIST NETWORK
800-THERAPIST
(800-843-7274)

135

SOURCE NOTES

FRONT MATTER
1. Laura Collins, *Eating with Your Anorexic* (New York: McGraw-Hills, 2005), p. 6.

CHAPTER ONE
1. Personal interview
2. Collins, p. 30.
3. Kidzworld, "Eating Disorder Awareness Week," http://www.kidzworld.com/site/p3155.htm.
4. Steven B. Halls, MD, "About the 'Metropolitan Life' Tables of Height and Weight," http://www.halls.md/idealweight/met.html.
5. Christopher G. Fairburn, MD, Overcoming Binge Eating (New York: Guilford Press, 1995), pp. 6 and 11.
6. Judy Tam Sargent, RN, MSN, *The Long Road Back: A Survivor's Guide to Anorexia.* (Georgetown, Mass.: North Star Publications, 1999), p. 33.
7. Aetna InteliHealth, http://www.intellihealth.com/IH/ihIH/WSIHW000/23741/23741.htm.
8. Carolyn Costin, "Activity Disorder: Too Much Little of a Good Thing," WebMD, http://my.webmd.com/content/Article/83/97765.htm.
9. Lynne Mordant, MD, "The Golden Girl," Lifelines Foundation.
10. Collins, p. 34.
11. Personal interview

CHAPTER TWO
1. Personal interview
2. National Eating Disorders Association, "Statistics: Eating Disorders and Their Precursors," http://www.nationaleatingdisorders.org/p.asp?WebPage_ID=325&Profile_ID=41138.
3. WebMD, "Disordered Eating Past and Present," http://www.webmd.com/content/Article/83/97755.htm?pagenumber=6
4. Ron Van Deth and Walter Vandereycken, "Miraculous Maids? Self-starving and Fasting Girls," *History Today* 43, August 1993, p. 37, http://www.eatingdisorderresources.com/articles/historytoday0893.htm.
5. Daniel DeNoon, "Reports: Olsen Twin Fights Eating Disorder: Are You—or Your Child—at Risk?" WebMD, June 23, 2004, http://www.webmd/content/article/89/100235.htm.
6. Carolyn Costin, "Assessing the Situation," WebMD, http://www.webmd.com/content/article/83/97769.htm.
7. National Eating Disorders Association.
8. National Eating Disorders Association.
9. Kristin Leutwyler, "Treating Eating Disorders: The Discovery of Two New Hormones Gives Researchers Food for Thought," Scientific American, March 2, 1998, http://www.sciam.com/article.cfm?articleID=000F1938-5721-1CE0-B4A8809EC588EEDF&sc=I100322.
10. Marlene Smits, "Anorexia 'Has Genetic Basis,'" BBC News, October 7, 2001, http://news.bbc.co.uk/2/hi/health/1575523.stm.
11. CNN, "Research Could Shed Light on Eating Disorders," December 10, 2004, http://archives.cnn.com/2002/HEALTH/conditions/12/10/otsc.anorexia,antibodies/index.html.
12. CNN, "Researchers Link Brain Chemical and Anorexia," July 14, 2005, http://www.cnn.com/2005/HEALTH/conditions/07/14/anorexia.brain.ap/index.html.

13. National Eating Disorders Association.
14. Something Fishy, Website on Eating Disorders, "Genetics and Biology," http://www.something-fishy.org/isf/genetics.php.
15. National Eating Disorders Association.
16. Something Fishy, Website on Eating Disorders, home page, http://www.something-fishy.org
17. Personal interview
18. Remuda Ranch, "Programs for Eating Disorders," http://www.remuda-ranch.com.
19. Kidzworld, "Eating Disorder Awareness Week."
20. Dorrie McCubbrey [What publication?]
21. Personal interview

CHAPTER THREE
1. Personal interview
2. Debra Katzman, MD, and Leora Pinhas, MD, *Help for Eating Disorders* (Toronto: Robert Rose Publishing, 2005), p. 88.
3. Samantha Stear, MD, "Disordered Eating," BBC http://www.bbc.co.uk/health/healthy_living/fitness/energy_disordered.shtml#osteoporosis.
4. Katzman and Pinhas, p. 83.
5. Ibid., p. 76.
6. Ibid., p. 82.
7. Andrea Braslavsky, "Eating Disorders Don't Discriminate," WebMD, June 6, 2000, http://www.webmd.com/content/Article/25/1728_58223.htm.
8. Braslavsky.
9. Anorexia Nervosa and Related Eating Disorders, Inc., "Males with Eating Disorders," http://www.anred.com/males.html.
10. Personal interview
11. Personal interview

CHAPTER FOUR
1. Personal interview
2. Something Fishy, home page.
3. Sargent, p. 97.
4. Jim Morelli, "Teen Eating Disorders, Psychological Problems Often Hand-in-Hand," WebMD, December 4, 2000, http://www.webmd.com/content/article/29/1728_65681.htm.
5. Empowered Parents, "Statistics," http://www.empoweredparents.com/pages/statistics.htm.
6. Kidzworld.
7. Personal interview
8. Personal interview
9. Personal interview
10. Personal interview
11. Sargent, p. 138.
12. Personal interview
13. Anna Paterson, http://www.annapaterson.com.
14. MSNBC, "Anorexic Student Denied Valedictorian Title," http://www.msnbc.msn.com/id/7884243/
15. Healthy Place, Eating Disorders Community, "Eating Disorders: Becoming 'the Best Anorexic Ever,'" http://www.healthyplace.com/Communities/Eating_Disorders/anorexia.asp.
16. Personal interview
17. National Eating Disorders Association, "Eating Disorders Are Illnesses, Not Choices: Survey Shows Americans Agree," www.nationaleatingdisorders.org/p.asp?WebPage_ID=807.

CHAPTER FIVE
1. Personal interview
2. Bodybody Project, "You Can't Tell by Looking," http://www.bodybodyproject.com.
3. Personal interview
4. The Elisa Project, "Elisa's Story," http://www.smu.edu/eating_disorders/elisastory.asp.

INDEX

ABOUT THE AUTHOR

TAMRA ORR is a full-time writer living in the lovely Pacific Northwest. She has written more than fifty nonfiction books for kids, teens, and their families, including *America's Best Colleges for B Students, The Parent's Guide to Homeschooling, The Biographical Dictionary of Notable Hispanic Americans, Extraordinary Essays,* and *School Violence: Halls of Hope, Halls of Fear.* Orr attended Ball State University and graduated with a degree in secondary education and English and a minor in public health and safety.

Orr has a strong interest in issues that apply to today's young people. Eating disorders equally baffle and intrigue her as she recognizes how important weight issues are in today's culture. Speaking with the people who told their stories for this book was a sobering and profound experience for her.

In addition to spending hours a day at her keyboard, Orr likes to spend time exploring the area with her family. She has four children, ranging in age from ten to twenty-two, and along with her husband of twenty-four years, they spend as much time at the Pacific Coast as possible. No matter how many trips they make, they always see something new. In her limited free time, Orr reads as much as her family and work will allow and takes at least a couple of minutes a day to admire the mountains in the distance.